Damn English!

Gary Sherbell

Black Rose Writing | Texas

©2025 by Gary Sherbell
All rights reserved. No part of this book may be reproduced, stored in a retrieval system or transmitted in any form or by any means without the prior written permission of the publishers, except by a reviewer who may quote brief passages in a review to be printed in a newspaper, magazine or journal.

The author grants the final approval for this literary material.

First printing

This is a work of fiction. Names, characters, businesses, places, events, and incidents are either the products of the author's imagination or used in a fictitious manner. Any resemblance to actual persons, living or dead, or actual events is purely coincidental.

ISBN: 978-1-68513-610-9

Library of Congress Control Number: 2025933750
PUBLISHED BY BLACK ROSE WRITING
www.blackrosewriting.com

Printed in the United States of America
Suggested Retail Price (SRP) $17.95

Damn English! is printed in Garamond

*As a planet-friendly publisher, Black Rose Writing does its best to eliminate unnecessary waste to reduce paper usage and energy costs, while never compromising the reading experience. As a result, the final word count vs. page count may not meet common expectations.

Praise for
Damn English!

"This book will have a quite broad audience... Gratifying level of surprises and loving twists on usage... Nice range of humor, from slapstick to self-reflective."
–**Sue Ducharme, TextWorks**

"*Damn English!* is lots of DAMN FUN!"
–**Walter M. Mathews, creator of *Potpourri***

"A total hoot that had me grinning throughout...a delectable dish to savor and enjoy."
–**Sandra Coopersmith, writer, editor and cartoonist**

"Gary Sherbell knows how to get you laughing from the first page and keep you in hysterics for the entire book. In *Damn English*, Mr. Sherbell takes you on a journey through words and language: the good, the bad and the really ugly things we humans say."
–**D.B. Gilles, NYU Screenwriting Professor**

"Gary, this book was a charmer. I laughed, I learned. Thanks so much for the opportunity."
–**Lauren Grodstein, novelist and professor of English at Rutgers University**

"A light-hearted, witty and insightful take on the oddities, inconsistencies and idiosyncrasies of American English. You won't be able to put it down and you won't want to either."
–**Timothy Jay, Professor of Psychology at the Massachusetts College of Liberal Arts**

DEDICATED TO:

SAMUEL CLEMENS, who inspired me with perhaps the funniest essay ever written on language: *The Awful German Language*;

AND TO:

GEORGE CARLIN, who, more than any other modern-day comic, turned me on to the humor potential in language.

WARNING:

Certain portions of this work might not be suitable for persons under the age of 18.
On the other hand, the humor in certain other portions might strike some mature readers, mostly over 20, as a tad too juvenile for their reading tastes.
Therefore, the ideal reading age for this book is: 19.

Damn English!

INTRODUCTION—NOT A PREFACE

First off, what you are now reading (or skimming, whatever) is properly categorized as an "Introduction". It is definitely NOT a "Preface".

I used to think that the two were synonymous, and that together they constituted yet another egregious example of needless confusion in our wonderful English language. (For a big spiel on this very topic—redundant words and expressions—see the section *Double Talk*.)

Believe me, I'd have been only too happy to begin this book with a thematic bang: an expose of a significant English glitch, solidly illustrating the book's anti-English-language theme.

Alas, I am unable to do so. I searched "Introduction vs. Preface" on the web and, by golly, there *is* a difference between the two. And what you are now reading (or skimming, whatever) is no doubt an example of the former, not the latter, in that it provides basic information about the book's contents, as opposed to merely delving into such topics as: why I wrote it, or my methodology, or qualifications.

Except that... hmmm... now that I think of it... the initial four paragraphs of this Introduction (above) do kind of operate as a "preface" ... *to the Introduction itself*. Perhaps this portion even deserves its own title, as such: "Intreface"? Oh well, too late, I suppose, to formally insert that title now. Moving on, then, to the start of the actual Introduction...

... Which, as I said, is obliged to explain this book's contents and themes. The title already gets you started on that: it tells you that it's a critique of English. I can now be more specific: it's all about how dumb, foolish and frustrating English can sometimes be (the language, not the people.) You know what? I can be even more colorful in that description: it's all about English, from the asinine to the moronic to the zany.

Now, I did say that enlightening readers on *why* the author wrote a book is more properly in the domain of the *Preface* than the Introduction; but where is it written that an Introduction can't also digress into such a related topic? The answer: nowhere.

So I digress: *do* I have any purpose in writing this book, other than—oh, I don't know—the obvious one of amusing readers and thereby spurring vigorous sales which will throw off hefty royalties? Beyond what I've already received as an advance?

As a matter of fact (well, not *fact*, actually, since I can't prove it) I do have a higher purpose: to compassionately impart to all those struggling to learn English—and all those who grew up speaking it but nevertheless are still struggling to *use* it—that *you are not alone*.

Indeed, I sympathize with all such sufferers *because I myself remain one*. That's right, me, the author of a book about English, who was born and raised in the U.S.A. and whose very first words were in English. You know which ones I mean: mama, dada, eat and poop.

Just one contemporary case in point: my never-ending struggle to properly spell "recommend". I never seem to get it right on the first attempt: one "C" and one "M"? Two "Cs" and one "M"? One "C" and two "Ms"? Two "Cs" and two "Ms"? Even now, to write it for this Introduction, I was forced to go through my standard correct spelling protocols: I typed the word in and, as usual, I got a squiggly red line underneath (at least, that's how it works in Microsoft Word), warning me of a spelling error above, requiring me to vary the quantities of Cs and Ms until I finally hit on the right combination of each so the red line would go away. Such are the time-consuming remedies we are forced to employ to counter English frustrations.

(If any of you readers/skimmers have been having the same experience with "recommend", I'd like to hear from you. You can email me at: garysherbell @ gmail.com.)

But my "higher purpose" with this book (if I may immodestly suggest having more than one) goes well beyond merely giving emotional comfort to English learners and users; it's also my lofty aim to *ease* their suffering by identifying the damn language's atrocities, along with, in many cases, offering appropriate recommendations (yes, that word, again) for change.

I can hear you already with that biting contemporary sarcasm: Good luck with that! I don't entirely disagree with such a pessimistic prognostication. But whatever the prospects of my language improvement goals, you certainly can't deny that they are noble.

My original intention was to end the Introduction here. But my editor at the publisher saw it differently; she thought the Introduction to this point wasn't "meaty" enough, and that I should "beef" it up by going into the origins of English—indeed, into the origins of *language itself*. "First things first," she said, in furtherance of her cause (apparently oblivious to my lampooning that very expression, in the book, in the section *Super Duh*.)

I went on to point out that: the origin of English (and language generally) has nothing whatsoever to do with the themes of this book; that if readers were truly interested they could do an internet search of their own on the subject; that from what I knew, such searchers would find that even linguistic scholars are hotly divided on the issues; and that for sure, I myself don't qualify as one of them. In sum, I didn't see the point in my putting in my own two cents on the subject.

[In the interests of padding this Introduction, permit me to now digress on the expression I just employed: Have you noticed that when you offer your own thoughts on a subject, you offer *two* cents worth? But that when you ask for someone else's thoughts, it's "a *penny* for your thoughts"? In other words, we tend to value our own thoughts as being worth TWICE as much as other people's thoughts? I know, a penny difference might not seem like alot (see my dissertation on the proper spelling of "a lot") but it's the *ratio* that counts. Besides, it really does add up—especially when you consider how far more often we barge in with our own unsolicited thoughts than respectfully request the thoughts of others.]

Now, back to my editor and me, and our creative differences. We were kind of at an impasse—but it all worked itself out just fine, when serendipitously, she came up with a marketing gimmick which, as it turned out, needs to be addressed in this Introduction. She proposed that we give advance copies of the book to six individuals from around the world and then get early feedback from them which could be used to promote the book.

I came back with the idea that I could actually *address* these six throughout the book (not by name, of course—which I wouldn't be told, anyway.) My purpose: mostly to guide them in their responses. She agreed and we both further agreed that if I were to address them, then for the benefit of the readers I needed to at least generally describe the six and perhaps add a word or two on when and where they like to read. Here then are the six:

1. A RETIRED NEW YORK CITY JUDGE, divorced, Jewish. He reads all day, everywhere and anywhere, now that he has the time.
2. A LOS ANGELES PLAYWRIGHT, widowed, African-American. She likes to read on her back porch, after breakfast, before she gets down to the hard work of writing.
3. A 25-ISH BLOND MIAMI MODEL, "beautiful" by her own description, who likes to read while sunning herself *au naturel*[1] on a clothing optional beach.
4. A 35-ISH LIVERPOOL DETECTIVE SERGEANT. A bachelor, who likes to read, or at least appear to be reading, to attract more erudite female companionship, while sipping beer in a pub.
5. A WEALTHY HONG KONG BANKER, middle-aged, fluent in English, who likes to read books in English, while in bed at night, to his much younger second wife, who's from Shanghai, to teach her English.
6. A 40-ISH SHEEP-HERDER'S WIFE, living in the outskirts of Melbourne, who, since she suffers from insomnia, especially likes to read late at night to help her fall asleep.

---

[1] I know, French, not English. Which I will use whenever it better fits the occasion than the English alternative. What counts is which offers the best description, *n'est-ce pas?*

I think this Introduction has been sufficiently bulked up, don't you?

All right then! On to PART ONE! (Which coincidentally is titled, "DAMN ENGLISH". Same as the book's title, but without the exclamation point.)

If you've been skimming, time to switch to fully attentive reading.

PART ONE—DAMN ENGLISH

SECTION 1—SEEING VS. SAYING

Most English users—learners and long-time users alike—would probably agree that what's most vexing about the language is its spelling and pronunciation.

Isn't that right, Hong Kong Banker? You probably grew up learning English as a second language—given that Hong Kong, in your youth, was still a British colony—and I'll bet a pile of pounds that English spelling and pronunciation was and still is your greatest challenge.

Mainly because: English is not a phonetic language. What you see (i.e., in a word's spelling) ain't[2] necessarily what you get (as a guide to proper pronunciation.) And what you hear ain't necessarily so, either, as a guide to proper spelling.

And it gets worse. Often spelling does reasonably comport with the pronunciation, but you'll still get it wrong; the devil is in the spelling details. Take, for example, the previously mentioned word, "recommend". Even if, based on how it sounds, you've accordingly inserted a "C" sound and an "M" sound, in your written version, you could still easily go astray by getting the *quantities* of Cs and Ms wrong.

Mishegas, right Judge? A Yiddish word I'm sure you well understand—meaning craziness? Of the senseless variety?

---

[2] I know, improper English, but I'm aiming for a conversational style. Only problem is—as with this little ditty—it's at best unhelpful and at worst downright erroneous.

Sometimes the spelling pitfall isn't the *quantity* of certain letters but the *order* in which they appear. One such pitfall—more like a *landmine*—is the proper order of "I" and "E".

In fact, generations of English teachers have been so desperate to inject some order into the chaos, that they've even come up with rhymes to promote proper spelling—like the famed "'I' before 'E', except after 'C'".

Oh sure, there's such a thing as "exceptions which prove the rule", but here, the exceptions far outnumber the rule-followers. Like: seize, height, albeit, eight, weigh, neighbor, sleigh, forfeit, and last but not least, fancier and science, with "Is" *before* "Es", though *after* 'Cs".

Fellow word-smith, Los Angeles Playwright: your bailiwick is fiction, and you know fiction when you see it. Does not this little rhyme qualify?

So far I've presented only the tip of the crazy spelling iceberg, standing as an obstacle to all those who aim for smooth English sailing. Here's some more wacky spelling to ponder...

THE SILENCE OF THE "B" IN "LAMBS"

Obviously an allusion to the great film, *The Silence of the Lambs*, as a fitting title for a subsection pertaining to the plague of *silent letters* in English—letters which are inserted in a word but have no impact whatsoever on its pronunciation. Especially fitting here since "lamb" is one of those offending words, with its silent "B" at the end.

Given that a lamb is a young sheep, it's a word heard often in your workplace, I'm sure, Melbourne Sheep-Herder's Wife. Though I don't know how often you have to spell it. And I don't know how much you're bothered when all those lambs are not so silent.

The silent "B" in "lamb" is just one of thousands of silent letter additions in our delightful language. Letters from "A" to "Z". That's right, silent "Zs" too—as in "rendezvous". (Bet you thought I couldn't come up with one.)

In fairness to the Grand Old Language, there is an occasional method to this spelling madness—a useful purpose being served by the non-pronounced letter, as it helps to tell apart one word from another, at least when the words are seen and not heard. It's the addition of a silent letter which often actually creates many *homonyms*—two words sounding the same but spelled differently, and with different meanings. (See Section below for more on homonyms.)

Were you expecting me to now list them all here? NOT.

Which coincidentally is one of them: with a silent "K", added to "not", to help distinguish the written "knot" from "not".

But I will cite a few further examples of helpful silent letter additions creating homonyms: adding "H" to "our" to distinguish "hour" from "our", adding "K" to "new" to distinguish "knew" from "new", and adding "W" to "to" to distinguish "two" from "to"…

One should not poo-poo the importance of these silent letter comprehension aids. (By the way, for more on "poo-poo" see later section.) Just imagine if there was no "W" in front of "hole", to distinguish "whole" from "hole". Consider this possible exchange:

"Is it whole?"

"No, there's a hole."

"Wholly unacceptable!"

"I'm trying to fill the hole."

"The whole hole?"

"On the whole."

How confusing this would be, if spoken. At least, in written form, the visible "Ws" would facilitate reasonable comprehension.

On the other hand, we don't want to go overboard in emphasizing the comprehension benefits of adding silent letters. For example, I don't think it makes much difference whether the Queen is expecting a knight night or a night knight.

I can't leave this subject without giving at least some mention to the silent letter in the very title of this book: the "N" in "damn". And vitally helpful it is, at least for prospective readers of it. Otherwise, without the

"N", many such readers might mistakenly conclude that this book is about man-made flowing-water obstacles in the U.K..

NYMS-HOMO

Oh sure, we native English speakers all grew up bemoaning the plethora (though we didn't use *that* word growing up) of homonyms in English—you know, as I said, pairs of words pronounced the same, but with different meanings *and* spellings. (Just used one—catch it? "Know", homonymed with "no".)

Now, as you (also) know, I'm no linguistic scholar and don't pretend to be[3], and therefore have chosen not to explore the origins of English. Except for—so far—my barely touching on the subject by suggesting, above, that certain silent letters were added to words to create homonyms, for improved comprehension.

But since I have already "opened the door" to discussing the origin of damn homonyms, I will now demonstrate how, in some cases, I believe one homonym word actually arose, at its inception, as an offshoot from the earlier use of the other. Like:

+ Boar and Bore… and Bore
First came "boar", the word for the tusked mammal. I suspect that when a boar used its tusks, to do what we now call "boring", like when it stuck one into a fellow mammal, it was simply and initially called "boaring". But then along came an advocate of Intelligent Language Design, who noticed that there were other types of "boaring" coming into verbal use, like when a human made a hole in something, using a tool, so that a differently spelled generic form was needed. Hence the birth of "boring". But wait, that's not the end of it. For all this talk about boars and boring took its toll on fatigued listeners, who began to mentally feel what we now call "bored". Except that the ILD folks haven't gotten around yet to giving

---

[3] And even if I was, I wouldn't tell you. Who wants to read a book that's supposed to be funny, written by some boring academic type?

this new type of "boring" a spelling that differs from the one for the "boring" that means "hole-making". So while either type of "bore" is a homonym with "boar", they are not, strictly speaking, homonyms to each other—just varied meanings of the same word.

+ Whether and Weather
First there was "whether", another way of saying "if". But over the centuries—and the millennia—the biggest "if" that concerned people was whether it would rain or snow. "Do you know whether it will rain, Moog?" "I wonder whether it will snow, Oog." And so it went, and with the word "whether" being prominently featured in most of these precipitation inquiries, it was inevitable (wasn't it?) that the general name for these conditions would itself evolve from the word "whether", later morphing (following ILD input) into the differently spelled "weather", for improved comprehension.

+ Here and Hear
First, I theorize, came "here", meaning the location where you, the speaker, were. Eventually, when you wanted to communicate that a speaker was speaking loudly enough to be heard—in other words, that for all intents and hearing purposes he was "here", not "there"—a variation of "here"—"hear"—was adopted. Makes perfect sense to me; how about you? Liverpool Detective Sergeant: ready to exclaim, "Hear, Hear"?

+ Want and Wont
Full disclosure: I hate to use "wont". Okay, maybe "hate" is too strong a word; let's just say I have a *distaste* for its usage. A bit too pedantic for my tastes—in spoken as well as written English. Indeed, when I do sometimes feel compelled to use it, I tend to say it facetiously, as if I'm making fun of its stuffy formality. It cannot be denied, though, that at least "on paper" (that's right, when in writing) its use can have utility, since to "want" to do something, meaning "desire" to, can sometimes be decidedly different from what you are "wont" to do, meaning inclined to actually do.

So you want to know, which came first? My money is on "want".

Going back thousands of years, we knew damn well what we "wanted" to do, but once the mores, in particular the constraints of so-called civilization, kicked in, what we wanted to do started to take a back seat to what we may not have wanted to do but felt *forced,* or at least pressured to do, fearing social backlash if we didn't—still a powerful motivating force today. Hence we'd end up being *wont* to do (or not do) what we truly did not *want* to (or did want to) do. (Am I making myself clear? Gee, I hope so; I won't be repeating it.) It would be natural, under this freedom impingement scenario, that "want" came first, and "wont" followed into usage only much later, when people saw that their "wants" were being taken over by "wonts".

To be sure, I haven't examined anywhere near all the homonym combinations necessary to discover all those where one logically spawned the other. Perhaps, Los Angeles Playwright, you can come up with some more? Love to hear from you: garysherbell @ gmail.com.

As for you Judge, I can just feel your skepticism of my theorizing—as someone who, all your professional life, has had to weigh reliable evidence against rank speculation. Your thoughts on my approach are welcome. Same email address.

And as for you, Hong Kong Banker: a little task for you, right up your alley, keeping the accounts. Let's see, I "put in my two cents" on four homonym combo origin speculations. If my math is correct, that's a total of 8 cents. Record that please in my "two cents inputs account".

NYMS-HETERO

Now for your consideration, dear reader (that's d-e-a-r, not d-e-e-r) another type of damnonym word coupling: the *hetero*nym—far more worthy of linguistic damnation. Here, the two words with different meanings are spelled the *same*—only *pronounced* differently. As in "lead" (pronounced "LEED", to give direction to) or "lead" (pronounced "LED", the heavy metal.) Or "tear" (pronounced "TEER", the eye liquid) or "tear" (pronounced "TARE", to rip apart.) Or "close" (pronounced "CLOZE", the verb for ending something—like shutting a door) or "close" (pronounced "CLOCE", meaning near in proximity.) Or how about "minute" (pronounced "MINit", meaning 60 seconds), or "minute" (pronounced "myNOOT", meaning very small)?

At least, with its homo cousins, you can *see* the differences between the two words when you read them, thanks to their different spelling. And when they are spoken, well, your distinguishing between them is aided by the speaker's facial expression and mannerisms, and the context and the like. But with the heteros, while speaking and hearing them presents no comprehension problem, what with the different pronunciations, telling them apart *in writing*—with their identical spelling and the writer not present to shed further meaning light—is literally (pun intended) a disaster. About all you can count on to help you distinguish them is context. For the second time in this book: Good luck with that!

Perhaps the most notorious example of this linguistic atrocity: "read". Or do I mean—"read"? Precisely my point! Do I mean the present tense—or the past? Sorry, the spelling won't help—the spelling is the same!

As a matter of fact, I already used the word in this very discussion: two paragraphs above, first line… "when you read them…" Admit it: you had to spend a couple of seconds to figure out whether I meant "read" in the present tense, pronounced "REED", or "read" in the past tense, pronounced "RED".

As if this cockamamie linguistic quagmire isn't confusing enough, consider that when you say, "I did read", clearly referring to a past happening, you use the *present* tense pronunciation, "REED". And, when you use the *present* perfect tense, "I have read", it is the *past* tense pronunciation, "RED", which is correct. Yikes, what hath the language gods wrought?

This is no minor matter. Why, it must have happened *hundreds* of times over my lifetime that I read (RED) "read", and had to stop, for at least five seconds, sometimes more, in order to decipher, from the context, whether the writer meant "read-RED" or "read-REED". Perhaps over my lifetime that has added up to two, maybe three hours of wasted time that could have been better spent. Perhaps, for example, that would have been enough time to read (REED) an entire Sunday *New York Times*! (Okay, the first five sections, not including the magazine.)

Please don't defend English—and this heteronym debacle—by pointing out that it could be worse. You might say, what about "bore" and also "bear", for example, where in both cases the very same word has different meanings with NO different pronunciations, let alone spellings, to distinguish them. My response would be: enough with your linguistic whataboutism. The English heteronyms language gaffe is intolerable. Your argument would be plainly invalid (pronounced inVALid, meaning not valid, as opposed to "invalid", pronounced "INvalid", meaning someone who's sick and homebound.)

Can you believe that this travesty has gone on for so long—for centuries—with no one in a position of linguistic authority bothering to correct it? Where, in this case, were those promoting Intelligent Language Design? Not even one influential person has come forward to suggest adding, say, an "E" to the end of "read", to create "reade", for the present tense version? Not even someone from the Duane Reade pharmacy chain? For the free publicity?

Just as there is, now, a movement to combat climate change, there is a crying need for a movement FOR *linguistic* change. What's needed is a legislative solution. Just for starters a law which, as I suggested, would require the addition of an "e" for the present-tense version of "read".

The promulgation of any such law should begin, of course, with British Parliament—the legislative body of the land where the language all began. Then, if a law is passed there, it should be sent across the "Pond" for consideration by the U.S. Congress—the chief legislative body of the country with the most English-speaking people. The two bodies together would then constitute what I would call the English World Legislature (EWL). And if the law is also passed in Congress, why then it should be THE LAW for all English-speaking people in the U.S. and the U.K.. With the hope that it will be followed by all English speakers around the world—like you, Hong Kong Banker, and you, Melbourne Sheep-

Herder's Wife. Perhaps this EWL can bring some long-awaited order and sanity to the chaos and insanity which now prevails.

Judge, you're somewhat experienced in legal and legislative matters—as well as being a lifelong English user. What's your take on my proposal? Its desirability? Feasibility? Garysherbell @ gmail.com.

As for the rest of you readers (REEDers): I just hope that this little anti-heteronym diatribe of mine didn't *bore* you. (Sorry, you'll just have to figure that out from the context.)

SPELL CHECKS

… Wherein we recognize (in the U.S.) as well as recog*nise* (in the U.K.) that some words are properly spelled in *two* ways, yet both variations have precisely the *same* meaning and pronunciation. What—English learners and users aren't having enough problems already with the damnonyms? Do they need this added complication to bedevil them? L.A. Playwright: when you submit a play to a U.K. theatre, should you have to be subjected to the headachy decision of whether to stick with the simpler "dialog", more commonly used in the U.S., or go with the more cumbersome "dialogue", still preferred in the mother country? Liverpool Detective Sergeant: when a U.S. law enforcement agency asks for background information on a Liverpooler and you're tardy in your response, do you stick with "apologise" or switch to "apologize"?

As I've already alluded to, many of these spelling conflicts derive from differences between U.S. and U.K. usage. But these "across-the-Pond" variations are, I believe, smaller in number than those found right within the U.S., and within every English-speaking country. (I admit, just an intelligent guess on my part; I haven't actually researched this.) Look, for example, at all the dual spelling options found just in the letter "a": "ax" or "axe", "ay" or "aye", "adz" or "adze"… I'm going to stop right there with my point, I think, being made…

I don't see that these spelling variations offer any benefit whatsoever, except to torment English learners, and perhaps therefore help separate the A students from the B students (if it is still politically correct to enforce that distinction.)

One would think that this problem should also be submitted, for reform legislation, to my proposed EWL (English World Legislature). Fine, no harm in trying, but I seriously doubt whether any legislation would pass which limits spelling to one variation per word. I predict intense lobbying pressure standing in the way of any change.

Pressure from, say, Anglophiles, who want to preserve British alternatives, you're thinking I'm thinking? Well, if that's what you're thinking, you're *wrong*. For I believe the biggest lobbying pressure against any change would undoubtedly come from… SCRABBLE players!

Think about it… Suppose you're playing Scrabble and are holding an "ax" on your rack, and there's an open "e" on the board, in front of which you could put down your "ax"—with the "x" placed on a triple-letter box—for a point total of 26, what with the "x" worth 8. How would you react, as a Scrabble player, if a new spelling law outlawed "axe"—allowing only "ax"—which would deny you this 26-point opportunity? Now imagine you hold "adz" and there's an open "e"—with the "z" possibly landing on a triple, yielding a bonanza of *34 points*—but only if "adze" was still legal! How would you feel about that word suddenly becoming unusable? Or what if "ay" was outlawed, leaving only "aye"—so that you could no longer put a simple "a" next to an available "y" and then make a whole new word perpendicularly, starting with the "a"? "No way", I can hear the Scrabble lobby screaming, at such a disruptive spelling law proposal. Hell hath no fury like a Scrabbler stymied. One more time: Good luck with that!

ALOT (NOT A MISPRINT)

One of the good things about being the author of a book is that you have the freedom (within reason) to air your pet peeves. And the peeviest of all my language peeves—a.k.a. "Sherbellyaches"—is that "a lot" is "properly" spelled as two words, instead of one: "alot".

When I mention to people that "a lot", officially, in standard English, is spelled as two words, many officially tell me that I'm crazy, and that it's "obviously" just one word. Whereupon I am behooved to take them to the internet to prove "a lot" is the current proper written usage. Another way to prove the point is to type in "alot" in a document, after which Word will automatically "correct" it to the two-word format, "a lot".

Conceded: it's standard written English. But *should it be?* My proposed EWL should, and must, take this matter up.

Quite simply, "a lot", when meaning a large quantity of something, should henceforth and forever be spelled as one word, "alot". Here's why:

The second word component of this two-word phrase, "lot", supposedly refers to a definable amount, of large proportions, so that having one—"a"—of them in turn means a large quantity. Problem is, that unlike, say, "a dozen", which does refer to one fairly large, or at least definable quantity of something—to wit, twelve of them—"lot" does not refer to a specific amount which, to start with, is large. Instead, all it might refer to is a "set" or "group" of things—but in no particular quantity, which means it could be quite small in number. Or it could mean an area, such as a "parking" lot, which again can be of any size, not necessarily large. Or it can mean an undeveloped parcel of land—like the small empty "lot" on the corner where I grew up, which contained … absolutely nothing.

Because "lot" has no definable meaning, large or small, an exchange like this could never take place:

"Did you like the movie?"

"I liked it a lot."

"I liked it more than you. I liked it *two* lots."

While this conversation could easily take place:

"Did you like them?"

"Very much. I bought a dozen."

"I liked them more than you. I bought *two* dozen."

In short—and I chose that word advisedly—there is no reason to associate "a lot", i.e., "one lot", with a large quantity. Yet those who *hear* "a lot" *do* think of it as it *sounds,* as suggesting a large quantity, because they are processing it as one brand-new single word "alot" having its own definition—that is, "a large quantity". Well, if people are thinking of it as one word, and taking it as one word, then that's how it damn well should be spelled—as *one word*.

Whew! I know, I'm on a mission here. Apologies if you're a by-the-book (i.e., the dictionary) English professor, and are put off by my brash linguistic insurrection—*alo*t.

SPELL HELL

Sorry, but "Heck" just doesn't cut it. Or rhyme.

Knock Worst

"Phlegm" takes the honors. Two spelling atrocities in the span of just six one-syllable letters: a non-phonetic "ph" instead of an "f", to start, followed by a useless silent "g".

At least, there's linguistic, if not poetic justice here: the word stands for one of our more objectionable fluid emanations.

But don't expect any legislative reform here, anytime soon. As presently spelled, the word carries *14* points in Scrabble.

The Weirdest

"Wednesday", any day of the week.

Most authorities state the proper pronunciation as "Wendsday", which implies that the word is spelled with an "n" *before* a "d", though when reading from left to right, the "n" indisputably appears *after* the "d". So that the established pronunciation makes no sense *unless* we read the word from *right to left*—thus encountering the "n" before the "d". But reading it from right to left in turn makes no sense—*unless* "Wednesday" comes from... Hebrew? How weird would that be? (Not actually a question.)

Surely, Judge, you understand the point I'm trying to make here—about the etymological implications of reading from right to left. But do most other readers?

Perhaps I've been ignoring you, up to now, Beautiful Blond Buff Beach Babe? If I have been, then permit me to inquire: did you get that? About Wednesday? For if you did, then surely, so did everyone else.

Okay, BBBBB, sorry for the stereotypical assumption. Just because a beautiful blond model likes to sun herself, in the buff, on a clothing optional beach, it doesn't mean she's a bimbo, does it? Well, *does it*, Liverpool Detective Sergeant?

Ough!

And now, ladies and gentlemen, your attention please, to our center ring, for the Most Amazing, Inexplicable and Indefensible Instance of Wacko English Spelling!

I am referring, naturally, to the "-ough" word clan:

"Though" is pronounced "THO"

"Through" is pronounced "THRU"

"Rough" is pronounced "RUFF"

"Cough" is pronounced "CAWF"

And "Bough" is pronounced "BOW", as in "when the bough breaks"

Same "-ough" spelling, bringing up the rear, yet FIVE different ways to pronounce it. Is that, or is that not, enough (eNUFF) to drive an English learner up a wall?

Sorry to report that tough (TUFF) -ough spelling has even infiltrated *geography*—as illustrated by a joke, about a little, ten-year-old girl, who lives in the upstate New York small city, Poughkeepsie:

She came home from school one day, and said to her mother, "Mommy, Mommy! I'm having such trouble in school! Teacher wants me to spell 'Poughkeepsie', but I can't! P-O-K-, no P-O-U-K-, no –. See, I just can't!"

Her mother said, "You just keep trying honey, you'll get it."

So the little girl came home two weeks later and said, "Mommy, Mommy! I'm still having trouble in school. I *still* can't spell 'Poughkeepsie.'"

And the mother said, "Well, then I have good news for you. You won't have to spell 'Poughkeepsie' any more. We're moving!"

"Great!" the girl said. "Where are we moving to?"

And the mother said, "Albuquerque."

SECTION 2—YOU SAY AND DON'T SAY

... In which we examine the peculiarities of English *usage*.

SAME BUT DIFFERENT

I don't need to tell you that there are thousands of words in English which have the same spelling and pronunciation but varied meanings. Like: "buff", which can mean enthusiast (as in "history buff"), or can mean nude, as in sunning oneself "in the buff" at a beach. (Gee, I wonder why that example popped into my head.)

Most often, there is little potential for confusion; the context will guide you to the intended meaning. But sometimes the confusion is so problematic that it rises to intolerable levels, and the dual meanings cry out for reform.

Take, for instance, the word "funny". It can mean in the "humorous" sense, but it can also mean in the "peculiar" sense. And since you often can't tell from the context which meaning was intended, the use of the word can lead to confusion, requiring further clarification from the user. After saying, for example, "there's something funny about that guy", the speaker will far too often feel behooved to promptly specify with either "… and I don't mean funny-ha-ha," or conversely, "… and I don't mean funny-peculiar."

I don't know about you, but my time is far too precious to waste on constantly having to explain which kind of "funny" I had in mind.

A solution to this verbal confusion may lie in the fact that, ironically, a similar confusion revolves around the use of the word "fishy" which, like "funny", can mean "peculiar", or can mean "fishlike", as in a "fishy taste".

Suppose that, from hereon, "funny" shall mean only "humorous", not "peculiar", while "fishy" shall mean only "peculiar", not "fishlike". Then, "fishy" would be used, exclusively, instead of "funny", to mean "peculiar", when heretofore you might have chosen to use "funny".

But, some of you are asking—and I'll bet, fellow word-smith, L.A. Playwright, you are one of them—how to now say that certain fish food has a "fishy" taste, when "fishy" can no longer be employed to that end? Why, simply say "fishlike", which, in fact, has no more syllables than "fishy". Furthermore, how many times, in your lifetime have you actually used "fishy" to describe the taste of fish—which would be obvious, anyway, without your commentary? Alot less often, I'm sure, than you've said "And I don't mean funny-ha-ha."

LEGAL BROTHERS

The way we refer to family members can often engender confusion, especially when we don't take the trouble to state precisely what we mean.

For example, you can have three types of fathers: your natural, biological father; your adoptive father; or your step-father. And you can have one or more at the same time—even all three. But there's confusion only when you don't take the trouble to properly identify, by status, which you are referring to.

Not so with one other family personage: the *brother-in-law*. Since no word or words exist to clarify which type you mean. (Same for the sister-in-law, but to keep it simple, we'll focus just on the brotherly version. Please don't get all woke-riled up at me over this.)

By my count, if you are a male (again, to keep it simple), you can have three types of brothers-in-law:

1. Your wife's brother
2. Your sister's husband
3. Your wife's sister's husband

And, as I said, no word or words presently exist to clarify which sort you mean.

… Which can sometimes have calamitous consequences. Did this ever happen to you, Liverpool Detective Sergeant? A man—sorry, a *bloke*—is shot, and dying, and after you ask him who did it, he, in his last gasp of life, says to you, "My brother-in-law"? And maybe he's got one of each of the three types listed above? And maybe, anticipating the confusion, you hurriedly ask him, "Do you mean your wife's brother? Or your sister's husband? Or your wife's sis's husband?", hoping he'll be able to answer you before he croaks? Wouldn't it be easier if each brother-in-law type had its own unique name—say "Type 1" or "Type 2" or "Type 3"—so all the dying murdered man had to spew out was one of those brief add-ons?

Okay, maybe this precise scenario never happened to you, Liverpool Detective Sergeant, but surely you can see how improved brother-in-law status clarification could at least in theory enhance law enforcement—and the pursuit of justice?

If anything, in recent times, with the acceptance of gay marriage, familial nomenclature has grown even more confusing. Now you can add to the list of "brothers-in-law": (1) your brother's husband, and (2) your wife's brother's husband. Yikes—enough murder suspects now to fill out an Agatha Christie novel.

But I'm not through. I know you are going to, well, kill me for this, dear readers, but I am behooved to also mention, at this time, the ramifications of transgender transitions on brother-in-law status. For example, suppose that murder victim, naming his "brother-in-law" as his murderer, had a brother-in-law who transitioned to a woman—effectively now his sister-in-law; would his naming of a "brother-in-law" as his murderer still include the transitioner as a potential suspect? Hey Judge, care to weigh in on this one with a ruling?

A COUPLE PLUS

Don't get all excited, Liverpool Detective Sergeant—this isn't about what you probably are thinking it is.

My question, to all readers: does "couple" strictly mean only a quantity of *two*, or can the numerical concept also encompass a quantity of *more than two*—albeit small? Same as "a few"? Say 3? Or even 4?

This question has been prompted by an actual true story. A while ago, my girlfriend and I were buying cookies in a store, and after she asked for "a couple" of them, the store worker produced 3. She complained that 3 was more than the "couple" she'd asked for, but I defended his claim that three could constitute "a couple".

When I informed my girlfriend that—actually, when she *discovered* that—this section would be included in this book, she… "suggested" that I take the opportunity to put the issue to a vote of the readers. So would you readers kindly respond: with a YES if you think "couple" can include a small amount more than two, or a NO if you think "couple" is strictly limited to the quantity of two. Garysherbell @ gmail.com. I thank you in advance for your cooperation.

LEFT-RIGHT/LEFT-WRONG

In one of English's damn greatest oddities, the word "left" can not only mean more than one thing, it can, in effect, mean things completely *opposite* to each other.

Consider this scenario: A husband and wife invite two couples over for dinner, Jane and John, plus Bob and Barbara. After dinner, our husband, who has had one drink and one bite too many, goes off to the living room couch for a brief nap.

When he wakes up, first thing he does is ask his wife, "Who's still here?"

His wife replies, "Jane and John have gone, but Bob and Barbara are still here."

Whereupon the husband proceeds to sum it all up: "So the ones who have left aren't left, but the ones who haven't left are left."

The wife, just a tad confused, says "Ri-i-ght...", meaning "Maybe, I don't know."

Whereupon the husband went on, "I assume Jane and John went home. When they left, they went left."

His wife replied, "Right." This time firmly.

Leaving hubby the one now confused. Did she mean "Correct", or "No, to the right"? …

... A confusion over the two "rights", which, I know, should have been included in our previous discussion of the two "funnies" and the two "fishies". But too late. Let's not go back there.

Okay, L.A. Playwright, your turn: Did that husband-wife dialog ring true to you? Garysherbell @ gmail.com.

PUT: DO AND DID

That "read" has no differently spelled past tense is queer enough. But at least the past tense version is *pronounced* differently—RED.

Not so for a host of other English verbs where the past tense not only features the same spelling but also the same *pronunciation*. And perhaps the most ubiquitous example of this grand linguistic snafu is the verb "put".

Consider this very possible dialog exchange:

"When you come home, where do you usually put your hat?"

"I put it on the top shelf of the hall closet."

"Where did you put it today?"

"I put it on the top shelf."

You just have to know from the context—the question that preceded it—which tense that last "put" was in.

All well and good when the context adequately clarifies *and* when it's all about the innocuous—like closets and hats.

But what if it doesn't—and isn't?

Consider this scenario: suppose a guy (or a bloke, as you'd prefer, Liverpool Detective Sergeant) approaches a gal (or—bloke-ette?) in a bar (or pub?) and, getting right to the point, blurts out a pressing inquiry: "Do you put out?"

(Okay, I get it, L.A. Playwright, this kind of question, even by a shallow male in heat, is not common, okay not even likely—just trying to make a point here.)

Now suppose the lass begins to reply, "I put out—", and perhaps, right at that moment, our bloke's hopes—among other things—have significantly risen. But wait, our bloke isn't yet home free (that is, he can't yet be sure she'll be transferring to his home, or hers, at no charge) until she finishes the sentence. For if she goes on to say, "... one time, last year," implying a *past* tense "put", the bloke's hopes—among other things—will precipitously crash. Far more stabilizing would be her sentence completion with a stated frequency along the lines of "often", implying a more welcoming *present* tense "put".

For sure, the blokester would do better to wait until the sentence is completed before making any rash move with financial impact, like offering to buy her a drink, don't you agree, L.D.S.?

ONE OFF

Here's an oddity of usage: we never refer to the body's "loins", as a noun, except in the *plural*. One would never say, for example, "I touched his loin," but would instead say, "I touched his loins," even when the touching was confined to one side of the body, the left or the right loin.

Yes, "loin" is occasionally used in its singular form, but only in limited circumstances: as an adjective, as in "loin cloth", or as a noun, to describe a cut of meat—for example, as in "pork loin".

By the same token, "genitals" is almost always used in the plural—as in, "I touched his genitals"—even when there was a lone touch to just one genital. The singular form, "genital", is only used as an adjective; for example, "genital herpes".

This single-vs.-multiple confusion can have serious due process ramifications, especially in this Me-Too era. A woman might accuse a man of, for example, "touching my loins"—because that's the only way she can say it—when in fact the perpetrator only touched *one* loin, the left or the right, thus, effectively *doubling* the gravity of the offense. Same due process glitch when a woman, due to the linguistic parameters, is forced to accuse a man of touching her "genitals", when in fact there was only a single touch to one.

This threat to civil liberties must end. Accusers must be allowed to accurately characterize the magnitude of the improper touching by employing, where fairly applicable, the singular noun forms, "loin" and "genital". In the spirit of "No means no," the "plural form" should mean *only* "more than one".

Given the highly injurious due process consequences of this linguistic gap, reform measures addressing it should be a priority of my proposed EWL. Judge? Garysherbell @ gmail.com.

Melbourne Sheep-Herder's Wife: did reading this passage somehow help you deal with your insomnia?

ONE AND ONLY

On to the other side of the two-cent coin: *missing plurals.*

One goose is a "goose". Two or more are "geese".

Simple enough. Then why not the same formula for more than one "moose"? No matter how many there are, it's "(number) moose". Two, a hundred, a thousand… it's still "moose". Not "mooses", not "meese".

And this living creature isn't alone. There are also no plural forms, in English, for: deer, swine… and another which slips my mind… oh yes, salmon.

And, saving it for last, for it's naturally of special interest to our own Melbourner, there's no plural form for *sheep*—which her hubby herds. It's just "sheep", no matter how many. No matter if there are none. No sheep.

Yet there are plural forms for "sheep" in other languages. French, for instance, where the plural of "mouton" (sheep) is "moutons" (more than one sheep.) Why is this, I wonder. Did English sheep fare far worse than their French counterparts during, say, the Black Death, virtually decimating the English sheep population, so much so that there was no longer thought to be a need for a plural form? Like I said, just wondering.

I suspect that any language reform proposal, to supply these missing plurals, which is submitted to my proposed EWL, would this time have an excellent chance of passage, what with the strong lobbying support I'd expect from the powerful animal rights groups. Surely it's in the interests of such groups that we clearly depict the true size of the animal population.

LOCATION, LOCATION, LOCATION

No, I'm not talking about real estate.

I *am* talking about a word or expression which can take on a whole different meaning, depending on where you are when you say it. So be careful!

Hay vs. Hey

If you yell out "Hey!" it will almost always be taken as "Hey", not homonym "Hay", no matter which you intend. With one exception: If you yell it outside the farmhouse window after the farmer's wife yells to you, "Where do you want to do it?"

Kiss My A*s[4]

Most often employed as a hostile exclamation, of course. But it can be a quite endearing, even erotic communication, when directed at another person you are alone with in, say, a bedroom. Also helping to make the distinction is your saying it in a decidedly soft tone.

PLAIN… IN… SANE

No other way to describe the English debacle known as "Inflammable".

---

[4] Since we are, after all, on the subject of location, it should be pointed out that the location of the asterisk here makes no difference. Same meaning with "As*". And even "*ss", since only an "A" would make a word.

With very few exceptions, the prefix "in-", in English, means "not" what follows. "Incorrect" means "not correct"; "incomplete" means "not complete"; "inappropriate" means "not appropriate", and so on and on and on...

Which brings us to "inflammable". Since "flammable" means easily set on fire, "*in*flammable" should logically mean "*not*" flammable—that is, "*not* easily set on fire"—right? WRONG! "Inflammable" actually means the *opposite*—"easy to set on fire"—*the same as "flammable"!*

Welcome to the "poster-word" for *Damn English!* Flammable = Inflammable = Insane.

Gosh, I sincerely hope that no one has yet lost their life due to this reckless nomenclature—mistaking something as relatively safe from catching on fire when on the outside of the package it misleadingly states the contents as "inflammable".

Hong Kong Banker, I do hope that your young wife won't be unduly discouraged from learning English after encountering this particular language debacle. Indeed, think about entirely skipping this passage when reading this book to her at night.

SECTION 3—DOUBLE TALK

Our dear English can be an expressive language indeed—especially with all the varied ways there are to say precisely the same thing.

But however (see what I mean?) you *can* have too much of a good thing, for English—*damn* English—is littered with far too many duplicate ways to say something, without a whit of nuance to distinguish one option from the other. Thus making the task of learning and using the language that much more difficult—or hard, or tough, or laborious, or arduous, or onerous, or formidable or more easily said than done… Q.E.D.? (If you don't know what that means, see *Damn Latin!*)

There are two possible solutions to this schizo state of language affairs: (1) eliminate all variations but one; or (2) devise different meanings for each variation so that they all serve a useful purpose and it would therefore make sense to keep them all in standard use.

Below are some groupings of popular duplicative words. In each case, see if we ought to pare usage down to just one or keep them all in use but only after nuancing up.

SOME COUNTRY FOR OLD MEN

Three words that mean exactly the same, all referring to males of an advanced age: (1) coot, (2) fogey, and (3) geezer.

(Curiously—and technically not belonging in this discussion, because it does not pertain to duplication—these three words are *always* preceded by the adjective "old". This added clarification is completely unnecessary, since old age status is implicit in all three nouns in question. There are no "young geezers", or "young coots", or "young fogeys". Come to think of it, there are no "middle-aged" ones either.)

If I were forced to choose, and pick one of the three, for continued usage, while canceling the other two, I suppose I'd go with "coot" since, at one syllable, it's the shortest of the three. (I don't see any reason to favor either of the other two, do you?)

On the other hand, this trio would be a viable candidate for retention with specialization, given that, in modern times, we are living alot longer (80 is the new 70, and so on) so there's an actual need now for further categorization. Here's my specialization proposal:

"coot" shall apply to men aged 65 to 73

"fogey" shall apply to men aged 74 to 82

"geezer" shall apply to men aged 83 to 91.

And what about men over 91? Why, they can be conveniently referred to as "old" geezers.

WITH A LITTLE… TAD?... OF LUCK

If you're a fan of all this English language diversity, there's probably no better example you could point to, to make your case for retention, than the many different ways we have to describe small quantities.

There's the "bit" of course, and then there's the "tad", and don't forget the "smidgeon". There are also "smithereens", which things are sometimes blown up into, and the ever-talked-about "iota", of which there isn't even one, it's said, when there's nothing at all of something ("not one iota"). A close cousin of the "iota" is "bupkis", reference to which is also confined to when the quantity is zero ("you don't have bupkis".)

Still, if there is to be retention of all the options, there needs to be specialization. Here's what I propose to that end: to begin with, 1 bit = 2 tads, and 1 tad = 4 smidgeons (so that, if you do the math, 1 bit = 8 smidgeons.)

The other terms, though, are not as easily incorporated into this grid.

"Smithereen", for example, presents an extraordinary size comparison problem, since when there's an explosion, and "smithereens" are created, they apparently only exist in the plural form, so that there is no practicable way to compare a single smithereen to, say, a single bit or tad.

"Iota" presents a whole other type of comparison obstacle, for the simple truth is that *no one has ever seen one*. "Not one iota"—a stand-in for zero—is the commonly employed reference. Well, if no one has ever seen one, how on earth can we compare it to, say, a bit or tad? The same complication is presented by "bupkis" which also exists only to highlight a quantity of zero.

In deciding between "iota" and "bupkis": might there be a way to salvage the use of both, on the ground of unique specificity, since they are usually employed in vastly different contexts? "Iota" is used in a more opinionated exchange—such as in, "There's not one iota of truth to that!"—while "bupkis" is employed in a more personal, derogatory exchange, such as when one snidely says to another, "You don't earn *bupkis*!"

And then there are ethnic considerations. "Iota" is, of course, a Greek term. So if you're of Greek ancestry, and it's Greek to you, a preference for it, perhaps? And "bupkis" is actually a Yiddish term. Judge…?

FEMININE WHILES

With men essentially in charge of language creation, over the languaged millennia, until recently, it should come as no surprise that English is full of different words denoting women who exhibit loose sexual behavior. (Have men somehow been thinking that the more ways there are to describe something, the more you get of it?)

And so, beginning centuries ago, we have been linguistically blessed with such varied expressive stalwarts as "slut", "slattern", "hussy", "trollop"… And I won't even count powerfully descriptive options like "tramp", which have alternate meanings not pertaining to unbridled female sexuality. Nor will I include words like "prostitute" and "whore", which suggest a more entrepreneurial motivation for engaging in intimate behavior than sheer sexual fulfillment. (Note that I do not presently consider, as falling into this "entrepreneurial" category, women who accept free dinners and the like, or even expensive gifts, as accompaniments to the dating process. However, I am open to further discussion on this point.)

As to that fast four—slut, slattern, hussy and trollop—all of which mean precisely the same, we are again faced with the language improvement decision of whether to settle on one and chuck the others, OR to come up with nuanced distinctions. And once again I come down on the side of *in*clusivity, if at all possible.

I believe full inclusivity is entirely possible here, based on newly devised meaningful differences.

My first inclination is to pair each one of these four terms up with its own, exclusive-use adjective suggesting loose sexual proclivities…

And so, I have arrived at: sluts are "licentious", slatterns are "lecherous", hussies are "libidinous" and trollops are "lascivious". Nuance by individualized association. Now let me check these four out on the internet. Be back in a moment…

… Yikes! No way! These four adjectives all have virtually the same definition: "inclined toward frequent sexual behavior". Distinctions without differences. Mission not accomplished! Moving on…

Let's see if I can come up with some other way to pragmatically distinguish them…

… A-ha. I think I have a solution—more like a *formula*—for distinguishing between terms for fast women based on their upper torso attire preferences.

My focus is on three attire criteria: (1) length of usually exhibited front breast cleavage; (2) width of bare midriff usually exposed; and (3) width of usually presented "side boob"—i.e., the amount of breast usually exposed from the side. (Would you agree that in terms of allure, one inch of side boob is the equivalent of two inches of front cleavage and three inches of bare midriff? L.D.S.? H.K.B.? Even you, Judge?

[I am addressing not only the straight men out there, but also gay women who are motivated by a similar visual focus when evaluating feminine allure. Each to his or her or their own.]

Here are my proposed distinctions applicable to the fast four based on these criteria:

+ A *slut* will usually exhibit: more than 5 inches of cleavage; 1-1 and ½ inches of side boob; and 3-4 inches of bare midriff.
+ A *slattern* will usually exhibit: 3-5 inches of cleavage; ½ to 1 inch of side boob; and more than 6 inches of bare midriff.
+ A *hussy* will usually exhibit: 1-3 inches of cleavage; more than 1 and ½ inches of side boob; and 4-6 inches of bare midriff.
+ A *trollop* will usually exhibit: more than 5 inches of cleavage, ½ to 1 inch of side boob; and 4-6 inches of bare midriff.

Now, under my proposal, if a particular woman presents as sexually loose but based on the above formula just happens to—er, slip through the cracks [sorry], uncategorized, why, then you will simply employ the verbal default setting, and refer to her as a *wench*.

Of course, further tweaking of my formula will almost certainly be necessary, and to that end, I would welcome comments from all readers on this topic of vital linguistic importance. Garysherbell @ gmail.com.

In particular, Liverpool Detective Sergeant, I wonder how a focus on your part on the above attire criteria would clash with your preference (I am told) for erudite women?

And as for you, BBBBB: I look forward to your weighing in, honestly, on your attire of preference—when you're not on the beach, I mean. The naked truth, please? [NOT sorry.]

POND-ERING

(I believe I didn't previously make this clear when I referred to the "Pond": it means the Atlantic Ocean, the body of water separating the U.K. from the U.S.A..)

Divided by a Common Language

Fellow Americans, take note: if we'd lost the war for our independence, and Cornwallis hadn't surrendered at Yorktown in 1780-whenever, we'd probably all now be saying "lift" instead of "elevator" and "flat" instead of "apartment".

Admittedly, these little inconsistencies are far more often amusing than confusing. For example, I recently read Danielle Steel's *The Right Time*, wherein the protagonist moves from New York to London, and when there, orders "takeaway" food from a restaurant; but when she moves back to New York her boyfriend visits her with restaurant "take*out*" food. If the discrepancy had occurred in dialog/dialogue it would have been understandable, given the inconsistent cross-pond usage; but the discrepancy here was in Ms. Steel's *own words of narration*—without a word of explanation for the linguistically astute reader. Further admitted: the vast majority of readers probably did not notice the discrepancy and, if anything, Ms. Steel is perhaps to be commended for her consistency with local usage. ("When in Rome, write as the Romans do"?)

Here's a list of some of the most commonly used words which have a different counterpart across the Pond. The U.K. usage is listed first. (I confess, Hong Kong Banker and Melbourne Sheep-Herder's Wife, I don't know whether the U.S. or U.K. version is more often employed in your area—though I assume the latter. Perhaps you can enlighten me?)

In each case I have also added a note on which one I'd prefer—if that EWL I proposed ever got around to mandating a choice.

+ Takeaway vs. Takeout

As mentioned above. Prefer "takeout". One syllable shorter. Care to weigh in, Ms. Steel?

+ Torch vs. Flashlight

"Torch" could easily be confused with another device used to shed light: an actual torch, the one you set afire. On the other hand, "flashlight" is one syllable longer. Preference: tossup.

+ Mobile vs. Cell (phone)

Prefer: "Mobile". "Cell" alone is one syllable shorter, but "mobile" better conveys the concept of mobility. Plus "cell" can be confusing, like when the prison warden says, "No cells in cells."

+ Lift vs. Elevator

"Lift" has many other meanings, as a verb, and even as a noun could equally apply to any machine that does heavy lifting. "Elevator", on the other hand, applies almost exclusively to a contraption which takes you up and down in a building. Even though it's four times as long, in syllables, prefer: "elevator".

+ Underground vs. Subway

"Subway" is an elegant way to convey precisely what is going on here, combining the concept of "below" with the concept of "movement". "Underground", on the other hand, conveys only the "below" aspect. Into the bargain, it's longer. Sub-brainer preference: "Subway".

+ Petrol vs. Gas

"Petrol", derived from "petroleum", precisely identifies the source of the substance in question, while "gas", as we all know, can also describe other forms of carbon-based emissions. Yes, "gas" is nice and shorter—but only by one syllable. Strong preference: "petrol".

+ Flat vs. Apartment

"Flat", at one syllable, is alot shorter than the three-syllabled "apartment". On the other hand, what with it containing "apart", "apartment" does better convey the concept of a subdivided living space. And "flat" has many other meanings in English. On the other hand, all those other meanings pertain to "flat" as an adjective, not as contemplated here, as a noun. On the other hand, "flat" does not always accurately describe what it supposedly pertains to, since some residential units, which would qualify as "apartments", are in fact multiple-floored duplexes and triplexes—hardly "flat" in layout. Still, can't ignore the virtue of brevity. Preference: tossup.

+ Football and American Football vs. Soccer and Football
We simply can no longer continue to have American "football" actually being called "American football"—instead of just plain "football"—anywhere on the planet. If this usage conflicts with the U.K. preference for the term "football" to describe what Americans call "soccer", then something will have to give. In other words, English "football" will have to be officially renamed "soccer", in the U.K. itself. U.K.-ers will have to understand that there are consequences to losing a war, as happened when Cornwallis surrendered in 1780-whenever. Unfortunately, when the Treaty of Paris was signed between the two nations to end that war, neither football, nor soccer, was popular enough then to warrant consideration of the conflicting nomenclature issue. So it will have to be taken up now, belatedly, by my proposed EWL. With my preference clear.

And now, Liverpool Detective Sergeant, on to that pair of U.K.-U.S. word alternatives, at least one of which I'll bet you use every day. And I'll further bet you've been wondering whether I'd have the guts to include it. Well, in answer to your wonder, I do…

Bloody vs. F*cking

Why "guts"? Because, after all, "f*cking" is the gerund form of a coarse verb for sexual intercourse, unprintable in standard, polite venues. And it's my understanding that this book may be so categorized.

Of course, all such forbidden words *can* be printed in most mainstream venues as long as there is proper asterisking (or hyphenating) within the word—which I've done. (What—there must be a minimum percentage of asterisks in place of letters, which I didn't meet? Complain to my publisher.)

I would further point out that in any case "f*cking" here has nothing whatsoever to do with sex—it is merely a way to verbally emphasize something—with extreme intensity. Same as "bloody", as a matter of fact, which has nothing whatsoever to do with actual blood—the red liquid—and is used only for emphasis.

The essential difference between them: "bloody" is used almost exclusively in the U.K. (and countries that follow U.K. usage), and virtually never in the U.S.. (Occasional exceptions here might come from, say, U.K. expatriates or tourists. Ever hear a "bloody" or two, BBBBB, from an angry Brit tourist you rebuffed on the beach?) F*cking, though, is sometimes used, in the U.K., purely for emphasis, as an alternative to "bloody".

And useful these words indeed are to inject emphasis. See how much more to the point "I'm so *bloody* tired" is than a tepid, "I'm so tired", for conveying max fatigue. Same for "I'm so *f*cking* tired."

That's right, "same"—a perfect segue to what is in issue…

Remember, the title of this section is "Double Talk" and it's all about the problem of possibly unneeded multiple ways to say the same thing. So, for the betterment of the language, are we to settle on just one, for easier learning and usage? If so, which will it be: "bloody" or "f*cking"? Or is there a case for keeping them both? Within certain usage parameters?

You know where I stand on this issue: I am in favor of keeping all options open whenever possible—pro-choice, in other words. And following my thorough examination of various usages of both "bloody" and "f*cking", I am pleased to report that the use of each can, at times, produce awkward implications, such that it would be beneficial to keep the other option around for occasional pragmatic substitution.

For example, if you've just murdered someone, leaving the victim's blood on your shirt, and you later misplace the shirt, it would be unwise for you, no matter how frustrated you are, to shout out, in front of others,

"Where is my *bloody* shirt?" If you were among the listeners, Detective Sergeant, surely you'd expeditiously pounce on the loose-lipped bloke, wouldn't you. Much wiser for the perpetrator if he'd simply substituted with, "Where is my f*cking shirt?"

In a similar vein, you wouldn't want to shout out, in front of your wife, "Where are my f*cking keys?" when your wife not only suspects you have a mistress but also suspects that a key to her apartment is on your key chain. Good idea to switch to "bloody" keys, even if you're from the U.S. and heretofore unfamiliar with this usage. (Judge, ever preside over a divorce where the wife learned about her husband's mistress from a telltale key?)

Of course, when choosing between "bloody" and "f*cking" you can sometimes find yourself between a rock and a hard place. Suppose, for example, you've murdered your mistress and her blood is on your keys. "Where are my bloody keys?" can get you arrested; but "Where are my f*cking keys?" can get you divorced. Your choice will come down to this: who do you fear most, the police or your wife?

Those who work in the sex trade have to be particularly careful in the choices they make here, to avoid confusion. For example, say you're a pimp and you demand of one of your employees, "Give me the f*cking money." The employee could rightfully be confused: do you mean the percentage you are contractually entitled to from what she earned by practicing her trade? Or, do you mean the money you had loaned her the other day, which she had promised to repay—debt money—with "f*cking" inserted merely for emphasis?

If it's debt money you're after, the solution is simple enough: go with "Give me the *bloody* money." Which would leave "Give me the *f*cking* money" for when you mean trade money. But there is a problem here when you want to add emphasis to this trade demand. You have several options: one is "Give me the *bloody* f*cking money"; or if you wish to avoid any implication that a virgin was deflowered at the time, and are okay with the repetition, try "Give me the *f*cking* f*cking money", with the first "f*cking" added purely for emphasis. Or, if you don't like having the word of emphasis buried deep in the middle, losing much of its oomph, you can go with a complete relocation, as in "*F*cking* give me the f*cking money," or "*Bloody* give me the f*cking money."

If you're a pimp and your employee owes you *both* kinds of money, the permutations and combinations are legion. Here are just some ways you might demand both sums, with appropriate emphasis:

"Give me the bloody money and the f*cking f*cking money."

"Give me the bloody money and the bloody f*cking money."

"F*cking give me the bloody money and the f*cking money."...

Hey fellow word-smith L.A. Playwright, maybe you can come up with some more applicable variations?

Wait—before you go—here's one more example of why it'd be useful to keep both "f*cking" and "bloody" in linguistic play. Suppose you're a lady—or would like to be thought of as one—and some guy makes an apparent move on you, getting a little too frisky with the location of his hands. When you've had enough and vehemently interject, "Get your *f*cking* hands off me!", perhaps you are carelessly giving him grounds for a defamation action, with your implication that his ultimate goal is sexual activity—even though you intended "f*cking" merely as a word of emphasis. It might be wise here for you to switch from "f*cking" to "bloody", thus avoiding the sex purpose overtone—as in, "Get your *bloody* hands off me!" Similarly, when a creep you have absolutely no interest in bluntly suggests intimate union, it'd be legally advisable for you to go with, "Are you out of your *bloody* mind?"

Even in the U.S.A., BBBBB?

SECTION 4—DOUBLE TROUBLE

From duplicative *words* to duplicative *expressions*. With the same issue: one and done? Or variety is the spice of life?

WHO'S THE SMARTEST OF THEM ALL?

When you want to suggest that a particular pursuit is NOT especially challenging to one's intelligence, you say one of two things: "It's not rocket science, you know," implying that rocket scientists are a pretty smart bunch, or "It's not brain surgery, you know," implying, with equal force, that brain surgeons are likewise a pretty bright bunch.

Yet to this date, no one, with authoritative credentials, has come forward to definitively state—let alone prove—which set of smarties is the smartest in the land. Not one member of these two esteemed professions has boldly come forward to make such an immodest claim.

My bold claim—to paraphrase Lincoln: the English-speaking world can no longer remain half-pro-rocket-scientist and half-pro-brain-surgeon. It's time to settle it once and for all (and sorry for the cliché): who's smarter. What the English-speaking world needs NOW is an authorized *contest, Family Feud* style, with three rocket scientists competing against three brain surgeons. With a celebrity entertainer, perhaps a comic, acting as Game Show Host, standing in the shoes of the late Richard Dawson (minus all the kissing, please.) And let the games begin!—a purely mental slugfest, with one group or the other emerging as undisputed intelligence kings (or kings and queens, or how about just non-gender "royalty"?)

Caveat: No matter which group triumphs in the contest, there would still be times when it would be necessary to refer to the other group to make the same traditional point. For example, if the brain surgeons win the contest, and a subpar brain surgeon nevertheless bungles an operation, it would be inappropriate to say, "Well, he's no brain surgeon, you know," since he obviously is. You'd have to say, "Well, he's no *rocket scientist*, you know." And by the same token, if the rocket scientists win the contest, and yet one of our rockets explodes upon launch, we couldn't awkwardly say of the scientist at fault, "Well, he's no rocket scientist, you know..." Better to go with, "He's no *brain surgeon*..." And you don't have to be a rocket scientist *or* a brain surgeon to get my point.

EASY DOES IT

Another pair of redundant expressions: "It's like shooting fish in a barrel", vs. "It's like taking candy from a baby." Both of these well-worn maxims purport to describe something especially easy to accomplish. There does not appear to be a way to keep both in use simply by tailoring each to certain specific contexts; reducing usage to just one seems to be the way to go.

Which one to stick with? They are virtually identical in import; even in length they are nearly equivalent (9 syllables vs. 10); and both are more or less equally offensive politically (one fosters shooting animals and the other fosters child abuse.) None of these criteria therefore present a basis for whittling down usage to just one, going forward.

How, then, to decide between them? It appears to this observer that the most pragmatic course to take would be another contest. Here's how it might work: put ten babies in baby carriages in a row, each baby holding a piece of candy. See how long it takes a certain individual to grab all ten pieces of candy from the hands of these babies. Then, put ten fish in a barrel of water, then time how long it takes for this same individual to shoot dead all ten fish. Then compare the times. And finally, after generations of use of these duplicative expressions, we'd authoritatively know which task is easier to perform—and more worthy of remaining the expression of choice, to convey ease of accomplishment.

CAKE WALK

As an alternative to the gerund-verb expressions ("taking", "shooting") in the previous passage, there are two redundant *noun*-expressions which also mean that something is exceptionally easy: "A piece of cake" and "A walk in the park".

Deciding between these two candidates with a contest would be hopelessly impracticable, what with neither the size of the piece of cake, nor the size of the park, being specified in the respective maxims.

Fortunately, no such contest is probably needed here, to eliminate one or the other, since there is a basis for preserving the usage of *both*. Each expression caters very specifically to people who lead very different lifestyles: cake eaters vs. frequent exercisers, who would certainly eschew anything as unhealthy, in their diet, as sugar-laden cake. Those contemplating use of one of these expressions would naturally prefer the one which fits best with their lifestyle. Ergo the continued use of both.

On the other hand, some modest sweets eaters, who do also take occasional park walks, might prefer an expression which combines aspects of both: "It's a cakewalk." [There's a joke in there, somewhere. Still working on it.]

COULDN'T CARE LESS (NOT COULD ... DISCUSSED LATER)

Two expressions in high vogue nowadays to convey that one's level of caring is as low as it can get: (1) "I don't give a rat's a*s", and (2) "I don't give a flying f*ck". Together they imply that a "rat's a*s" and a "flying f*ck" are so utterly worthless, or nearly so, that your level of caring is for all intents and purposes infinitesimal. Far lower in caring degree than implied in the flatter "I don't give a sh*t", or "… crap", or "… damn", or "I don't give a [non-flying] f*ck", or the flattest of all, "I couldn't care less".

But before we move on to the issue at hand—which of these two verbal nuclear options to use and when—I must digress, at this time (since the expressions are before me now) to the topic of much greater relevance later in this book: do these two expressions even make any sense? How/why did they get into common usage in the first place?

In that first first place, what's so insignificant about a rat's rear end—as opposed to another part of a rat—that it aptly qualifies as the essence of worthlessness, as implied in the expression?

And in the second first place, what exactly is a "flying" f*ck, as opposed to a "bus" or "train" or "car riding" one, or a "running" or "walking" or "jogging" one? And why is it a stand-in for worthlessness when it actually suggests (to this observer) something of great value? A memorable achievement? Detective Sergeant? Assuming you do occasionally fly?

Excuse me for asking…

You can continue to ponder my challenging questions, if you'd like, but I am behooved to move on now to the issue of redundancy.

Since both expressions say virtually the same thing, we are once again forced to decide: do we get rid of one, OR do we find that there's a need to retain both, so that each can be used in certain circumstances where only that one would suffice?

Once again, I'm proud to be pro-choice. Pro-variety. For example…

Suppose you are addressing a group of animal rights activists. The last thing you would EVER want to include in such an address is "… I don't give a rat's a*s about…" Remember who you're talking to here: *animal rights advocates*. And the rat—though justly maligned in history for causing the death of millions of *humans* through the spread of diseases, like the Black Death, in the Middle Ages—is nevertheless, a *mammal*. And a *smart* one, at that—or why else would we keep on using rats in so many experiments, as proxies for humans? To avoid animal rights cancellation, you must NOT suggest that a rat, *or any portion thereof*, is worthless, nor, even worse, that you would cruelly slice off that portion, just to make your point. In this instance, you would be wise to substitute, "I don't give a flying f*ck". Justifying retention of that expression—just in case!

(May I ask, Melbourne Sheep-Herder's Wife: how ticked off would you be if someone substituted with, "I don't give a *sheep's* a*s?" I'll bet, a lot. Garysherbell @ gmail.com.)

Of course, "flying you-know-what" presents its own cautionary flags.

Suppose, for example, you are on an airplane, traveling with a lady, and you've already promised that lady that sometime later in the flight, when you're at least a mile up in the air, you'd be "doing it" together in the bathroom, so that she could be introduced into the so-called "Mile High Club" (which consists of people who have had sex while at least a mile up in the air.) If you now blurt out, even on an unrelated topic, "… I don't give a flying f*ck …", you could be sending her an entirely misleading message about your Mile High plans, suggesting that you are reneging on your promise, even if it was not in the least your intention by using that expression. Can you think of a better time to issue an immediate apology and switch to a still-acceptable "I don't give a rat's a*s"?

I know what you're thinking, Detective Sergeant: Suppose the lady happens to be an animal rights advocate? What then?

I'm one step ahead of you, mate. In that unlikely scenario, in which you can't use either of these two preferred expressions, you'd simply have no choice but to turn to one of those previously enumerated, yes flatter but tried and true, lesser-caring expression options. Try to convey, with added vehemence, what the words themselves fail to imply.

FROM BEGINNING TO END

At the Beginning

You're a guy, a dude, a bloke … You approach a woman seated at a bar, in a bar (or a pub.) You begin a conversation for the purposes of hooking up, or dating, or beyond. Are you: (1) "chatting her up", in U.K. lingo, or, in U.S.-speak, (2) "hitting on her", or (3) "coming on to her"? All three options mean virtually the same. Do we need to keep them all in use? Or just two? Or one?

You'd think I'd ask BBBBB to weigh in on this one, since for sure she's been on the receiving end of countless such solicitations, especially when she's been on the beach in her most comfortable manner of presentation. But I'm not. Almost certainly she'd stray onto how she fends off such approaches, while I'm more interested in the *linguistic* nuances.

So then—tackling the issue solely by myself (which I am obliged to do, anyway, as the author)—I must say that after careful consideration I prefer the retention of U.K.-based "chatting up" and the chucking of U.S.-based "hitting on" and "coming on".

As for "hitting on": fact is, in this Me-Too era, this is no time to be employing an expression which incorporates a term—"hit"—implying physical violence. An admission, as it were, that in merely *talking*, with a sexual agenda, you are engaging in an assault of a type which isn't yet but might well become physical.

As for "coming on", it suffers from incorporating "come", the same word used to describe the ultimate objective. Too close for initial conversation comfort?

Which leaves us, almost by default, with "chatting up". Non-violent and non-sexual. Well, except perhaps for that choice of the preposition "up".

At the End

Time has passed… That woman you chatted up in that bar or pub is now your live-in girlfriend, or maybe even your wife. But the bloom is off the rose. In fact, the rose is dying. And you're thinking of dating other women. (I'm posing the issue here from a man's point of view, since it is usually the man who engages in infidelity.)

What do we call what you are about to do? Do we call it "stepping out" (a term far more common in the U.K. and its linguistic cousins) or do we use the U.S.-preferred term "cheating"? Or is there a rationale for the continued use of both?

You're not going to like this, men, but I'm afraid I come down on the side of calling it "cheating". Sorry, but "stepping out" just doesn't cut it, from the moral standpoint, as nail-on-the-head "cheating" does. "Stepping out" should be, well, *kicked* out of usage.

Judge, I'm told you're divorced. Perhaps you'd like to share: Did it result from either you or your Ex cheating on the other? If it was you, did the infidelity occur only *after* you were virtually "separated" for other reasons—though still living together—and your "infidelity" began only *after* sexual intimacy had long been over? In which case your infidelity did not truly constitute "cheating", at least from the moral perspective?

… You know what, Judge? As you'd professionally appreciate, I'm going to *reverse myself*. I'm going to suggest that there's *still* a purpose to the continued use of "stepping out". That when the infidelity occurs only *after* the sex has long ago died out, so it no longer carries the stigma of immorality which would justify the term "cheating", then all you are doing is the benigner "stepping out" of your mutual residence.

BARRELS AND BALLS

While we are on the subject—more or less—of adultery: suppose you are in the divorce process, and your sleazy divorce lawyer, with the help of his/her sleazy x 2 private investigator, has been able to obtain pictures/video of your spouse cheating/stepping out/whatever. For the purposes of establishing grounds for a divorce (if necessary) or at least a superior financial settlement, would you say you have your spouse "over a barrel"? Or go with "by the balls"? Which means virtually the same?

Now, if you are a woman, and your husband is the adulterer, then "by the balls" would not only be anatomically compatible, it would inarguably express poetic justice — and be the inevitable usage choice. But if you are the husband and your *wife* is the adulterous party, "by the balls" would seem to be barred by anatomical reality, and "over a barrel" would instead be mandated (except in the rare case that your spouse used to be a man and has so far declined to finalize the transition.) All well and good, then, when your usage choice can be conveniently guided by the anatomy of the person you control. But which expression to employ when neither option can be ruled out? In other words, which one is to be preferred as the expression which best comports with a greater degree of control in actual practice?

Perhaps another contest would be productive here, to determine which expression, if either, ought to be preferred. To that end, the etymology of both would surely be instructive, if not determinative. I assume, dear reader, that you well know where "by the balls" comes from. (IF YOU DON'T KNOW, STOP READING RIGHT NOW; NOT JUST THIS SECTION BUT THE WHOLE BOOK; IT'S NOT FOR YOU.) The derivation of "over a barrel" is not quite as widely understood. Apparently, it is a nautical term, stemming from the disturbing fact that in less humane times a seaman being flogged for disciplinary reasons was required to receive his punishment while standing on a barrel. A proper contest, then, would be to have a man, one would hope a volunteer, subjected to a ball squeeze, followed by a flogging over a barrel, to see which encumbrance, if either, better motivated him to more expeditiously comply with a squeezer/flogger's request.

I know what you're thinking, skeptical reader, and maybe you're right: that such a test would never come off, since it would be difficult, if not impossible to find a man, a *testee*, who would dare volunteer to be subjected to such brutal assaults. Indeed, I actually think that the greater difficulty would be elsewhere: in finding a test*er*, in particular someone who would be comfortable with squeezing another man's balls. Still, no harm in trying, at this time, to conduct such a test. Are any of you willing to volunteer to be a testee or tester? Testee must have medical insurance coverage. Tester must have liability insurance coverage. Garysherbell @ gmail.com.

GET LOST

Our wonderfully expressive English language presents at least *three* satisfying options for dissing a worthy other by suggesting that he or she GET THE HELL AWAY:

- Go fly a kite.
- Take a long walk on a short pier.
- Go jump in the lake.

I don't think any progressive linguist would quarrel with my conclusion, in this instance, that all three should be retained, for usage at various times, when appropriate—given their richly varied recommended activities (flying, walking and jumping) and locales (near a pier or lake, or near a wide open area suitable for kite-flying.)

Still, I do believe that I have some useful advice to offer, which would enable more appropriate use of these expressions:

- If you don't want any serious harm to befall the dissee, don't command the dissee to go "jump in a lake" if he or she can't swim. Ditto for the use of taking a "long walk on a short pier", which would also culminate in the dissee's taking a water dunk. And, needless to say, one should never urge the "flying of a kite" during an electrical storm.
- On the other side of the ledger, if you want the diss to effectively communicate a vigorous level of hostility, DO NOT employ "go jump in the lake" or "take a long walk on a short pier" on a hot summer day—and especially not if the dissee is wearing a bathing suit (or less—a la BBBBB.)
- Still on that same side of the ledger, don't bother with "take a long walk on a short pier" with someone who's slow on the uptake and won't even get the diss—won't appreciate the implied risk. Perhaps with such a dissee you can modify the expression to "take a long walk on a long pier". Bland, yes, but at least it will get the dissee far away.

+ Still on that aggressive side of the ledger, the circumstance might arise such that just a single diss command does not quite do justice to the level of your ire. You might then want to consider combining two, as in: (1) "Take a long walk on a long pier, and then, when you get to the end, go fly a kite"; or (2) "Take a long walk on a long pier, and then, when you get to the end, jump in"; or (3) "Go fly a kite, and then, when you're finished, jump in a lake." If that's still not enough—and the dissee really got your goat—you might consider combining all three, as follows: "Take a long walk on a long pier, and when you get to the end, go fly a kite, then jump in."

Of course, all of these combined expressions require the time to fully communicate them that you may not have. Indeed, being in a hurry, you might not even have time to employ one of the *single*-expression options. In that case, you'll have no choice but to employ that ultra-brief but still quite effective "Get lost". (Given the title of this section, you knew that was coming, didn't you.)

SECTION 5—FOCUS FRACAS

Many of our favorite—

Oops! Just realized, plum forgot to include the deserving "Buzz off!" in the previous section, on "diss options". Please go back and insert it, by hand, somewhere, say in a margin, then return...

Now, where were we? Oh, yes... Taking it from the top...

Many of our favorite expressions are confusing due to their lack of specificity, and could be vastly improved with a sharper focus. Here's what I mean...

THE OLD COLLEGE TRY

Yeah, sure, ask someone to give that "old college try" max effort – but *which* college? Don't you think it matters? Aren't we entitled to know?

If the challenge in question is of an *intellectual* nature, you might want to more specifically direct, "Give it the old—try," inserting therein the name of a university widely known for its *academic* prowess. [You don't actually expect me to suggest a name right here and now, do you? And offend all those who went to some other top academic school? Especially while I'm trying to get this book published by a university press, and/or reviewed by graduates of many of these elite institutions?]

Similar advice when it's a *physical* challenge in issue: insert the name of a school which has produced far more than its share of *athletic* championships. [Again, don't expect me to actually suggest a name now, thereby offending the grads of all the other athletic powerhouses. Here I would run an entirely different kind of risk: of being punched in the nose by a complete stranger, just walking down the street—most likely a six-foot-four, 260-pound former collegiate left tackle.]

DOGGED

Suppose you want to say that someone works really hard, *i.e.*, "like a dog"? Doesn't it make a big difference which *kind* of dog you mean?

Do you mean, works like one of those indefatigable German shepherds, employed in such capacities as police dogs or seeing-eye dogs? Or racing greyhounds or sharp-smelling cop-aiding bloodhounds? OR, do you mean one of those dainty, pampered Park Avenue poodles, who do nothing all day except laze around, watching TV with their dainty, pampered masters? On the other hand, do you mean one of those rough, tough huskies, who put in at least a 40-hour week pulling those heavy sleds, in freezing cold, way up north? Or in the same locale, one of those St. Bernards who bring you brandy when you've had a ski accident or have been nearly smothered by an avalanche? At least, so I've heard? OR do you mean one of those tiny, oh-so-cutesy—and eminently unemployable—chihuahuas, who are afraid of a teenie mouse—indeed, the mere *shadow* of one?

Don't worry, Melbourne Sheep-Herder's Wife: of course I will now put in a good word for your faithful, hard-working sheep dogs, who are so helpful in the guarding and herding of sheep.

More problematic are those dogs used in fox hunting: the foxhounds and fox terriers. Sure their helpfulness can't be denied, and they *seem* to be working while chasing that fox around—but come on, can you fairly call it "work" when such a dog also seems to be having so much fun at it? When it's the *dog's* "sport" as well? Your call.

The usage bottom-line: instead of just vaguely saying that someone "works like a dog", rather say, better to your point, "works like a----", inserting the name of a dog which really does work hard—preferably one whose work closely mirrors the work of the human you are referring to. Such as when he or she helps the blind, or catches crooks, or races competitively, or sniffs for a living, or pulls something heavy, or supplies you with booze, or guards sheep, or chases foxes.

[Cat lovers: sorry if you've been put off by the above passage, in which I have lauded the work efforts of most dogs. But you have to admit: there's a reason why we say "works like a dog" and not "works like a cat".]

ABSENCE MAKES THE HEART GROW FONDER

… of *whom*? The Significant Other you've been apart from for quite some time? OR, the person you've now been spending alot of time with, in place of the Other? Be specific (depending on whom you're addressing, of course.)

UNDERBUSING

Say you want to convey that someone became a "sacrificial lamb", in that he or she was made to take the whole blame for some misfortune, at the hands of someone who was just as much to blame, if not more so. Accordingly we often say that the lamb was "thrown under the bus". Problem is, this ubiquitous expression never tells us all we need to know: was the throwee only moderately harmed by the thrower, or, was he or she truly devastated? In bus terminology, was the throwee "thrown under a *moving* bus", or merely "thrown under a *parked*" one? Makes a huge difference—both in the real vehicular world, and when metaphorically describing a blame shift. Next time you use this one, be specific: parked or moving?

BARN TARGETS

So now you aim to badmouth someone's aim and you've decided to go with, "He couldn't hit the broadside of a barn". And you're expecting the listener to glean from that alone that the shooter's aiming abilities are something awful? Even though you haven't supplied such critical details as: (1) how far away the barn is, (2) how big the barn is, height and length, on the side facing the shooter, (3) how light out it is, (4) whether the shooter would be using a rifle or a pistol, and (5) whether, if a rifle, it had a telescopic sight? For example, if you really want to trash someone's aim, you might further specify with: "He couldn't hit the broadside of a 50-foot by 20-foot barn, just 10 feet away, in broad daylight, using a scoped rifle." Remember to incorporate these defining details next time y'all shoot your mouth off 'bout some other dude's poor aim, using barn talk.

DISARMING

The next time a pugnacious braggart challenges you with the assertion, "I can beat you with one arm tied behind my back," and you're not looking for a fight, try retorting, at first, by exposing the claimant's woefully inadequate specificity. Inquire thusly: "Are you a righty or a lefty? And which arm are you planning to tie behind your back—your left or your right?" Obviously you're entitled to know these relevant details before you reply to the challenge. Your adversary just might find your retort disarming.

BOOKIES

Often someone will say that he or she "goes by the book", or someone will even exhort you to follow that familiar prescription. But rarely, if ever, will the bythebooker specify *what* book he or she had in mind for us to be guided by. Obviously, books can vary greatly in their themes and messages, not to mention quality. Therefore, the next time you are thus exhorted, illustrate this contrary point of view—and the need for specificity—by asking the exhorter, "Which book do you mean? Do you mean…

- The *Bible*? Or *Fifty Shades of Grey*?
- *Profiles in Courage*? Or *Mein Kampf*?
- *How to Win Friends and Influence People*? Or *Damn English!*?"

MOMENTOUS

After you make a request for assistance, you will often hear in response, "In a moment," and are left to wonder: precisely—or even roughly—how long will that waiting time be?

The responder very possibly didn't have any idea of how much time he or she would actually need. Or the responder might have had an approximate idea—but didn't say. Which wouldn't entirely have been the responder's fault—for the unfortunate reality is that the English language had left him or her little descriptive choice. For there simply are no "subcategories" for "moment".

This needs to change—immediately, not some moments from now. We should no longer be limited in our usage to just "in a moment" when the response time—which the responder could reasonably estimate—could be anywhere from 5 seconds to multiple minutes. Note that when a responder is fairly sure that his or her time needed will be around a minute, "one minute" is a doable and effective response. There's no reason we cannot be as effectively precise when we respond in "moments".

Here's my proposal:

If you think you'll need anywhere from 5 to 10 seconds, respond "one moment".

If you'll need 11-20 seconds, respond "2 moments".

If you'll need 21-40 seconds, respond "3 moments".

If you'll need 41-59 seconds, respond "4 moments".

If you'll need more than 1 to 1 and ½ minutes, respond "5 moments".

If you'll need 1 and ½ to 2 minutes, respond "6 moments".

If you'll need more than 2 minutes, respond, "In a while."

SECTION 6—AS TIME GOES BY

Don't play it again, Sam… or say it again, either.

We (actually, just me) now turn to expressions the usage of which has come and gone. Or should have. But old language habits die hard…

OLD MACDONALD *HAD* A FARM

In the early days of the 20th Century, the U.S. was still predominantly agrarian, with—what?—90 percent or so of the population living and working on farms. And the language usage employed then reflected familiarity with that life style. Especially in the case of idiomatic expressions.

Though times have radically changed—and old Macdonald's grand and great-grandchildren are now toiling as lawyers, accountants and authors of non-fiction books—the language in use has barely budged from its agrarian roots. By dint of habit, dozens of expressions which arose in that farmy era are still made use of which we barely understand the derivation of. But if you don't understand how an expression came about in the first place, how can you truly appreciate its meaning, and properly employ it?

Axes to Grind

Oh sure, most users kind of know what this familiar one means, even though they've never actually held an axe in their hands, let alone ground one down for sharpness. I doubt most people have ever even *seen* an axe get ground. And yet we expect youngsters first learning the language, and foreign folks learning it as a second language, to jump right in and employ an expression like this, without the slightest notion of what axe-grinding is all about? Hong Kong Banker, you're trying to teach English to your young wife from Shanghai. If she didn't grow up on a farm in Shanghai would you really expect her to readily take to this idiom?

English speakers of the world: can't we put our heads together and come up with another expression, with contemporary roots, which adequately conveys "having an ulterior motive"? One equally sharp?

Beware Them Axe-murderers!

When we caution someone to remember to keep that door locked or window shut, what potential evildoer do we invariably warn that person of? Why, the *axe*-murderer, of course! Even though to my knowledge no one has actually used an axe to murder anyone in the U.S. since Lizzie Borden used that tool to carry out the murder of her parents in 1892! And in any case she was *acquitted* on that charge! So who knows if she actually did it! And secondly in any case she lived with her parents, so she was hardly the *outside-intruder* axe-murderer we are oft warned of!

What about, you might say, in the movie *Fargo* (based on a true story) wherein one kidnapper-murderer kills the other, in a rural environment, using a long-handled axe? I retort: again, this was not an instance of the feared axe-wielding *outside intruder* posing a danger to a complete stranger. Admittedly, though, as demonstrated in this film, the axe does have one significant advantage over a gun or any other weapon: when it is your intention to fit the remains of your victim into a wood chipper.

Indeed, of all the persons with murderous inclinations living in our midst right now, as I write, what percentage even *possess* an axe as a weapon to potentially make use of? Miniscule, I'm sure. Probably even less in the U.K., am I right, Detective Sergeant?

While the continued use of this expression might not present any serious learning or comprehension issues as does "axe to grind", the use of it carries far more harmful *social* consequences: by focusing on the danger of an axe-murderer, which listeners know to be a rare occurrence, if not altogether non-existent, we are in fact lulling these citizens into a false sense of security, thus making them even *more* at risk from a murder brought about by a commonplace contemporary weapon.

Coming Cows

I have no idea "when the cows come home". Neither do any of the 98 percent of other Americans who have never lived on a farm, let alone a dairy farm. So why should I and these others continue to use an expression we don't fully understand? Oh sure, I get that it suggests somewhat later in the day, but how much later? When it's still light out, in the early evening, in the summertime? Don't know.

What we urbanites would appreciate is an alternative expression which better correlates with our urban experience. How about, "When the rats go back to their garbage cans," or "When the roaches return to their wall cracks"? Just two which readily come to mind.

Sow Wow

Of course, not every creaky-old farmy expression is unable to do its communication duty in more modern times, even for urban types who haven't the slightest idea what the expression is getting at in the real world.

For example, in the movie *The Graduate*, young Ben Braddock, played by Dustin Hoffman, after famously receiving one-word career advice from an adult—"Plastics!"—shortly thereafter receives further advice from another adult: the farmy "Sow your wild oats", which he fully gets the gist of, and proceeds to follow, even though, as an L.A. born-and-raised city boy, he hasn't the foggiest notion of what it means, agriculturally, to "sow wild oats". And how wild are the oats he goes on to sow? Get this: he begins his sowing with the wife of the man who gave him the advice! And to further demonstrate his utter wildness, he goes on to sow with none other than the *daughter* of this man—and of the woman with whom he first sowed! All that without having one iota of knowledge on how oats are actually sowed!

FOOD FOR THOUGHT

Many expressions stem from eating practices. And with the change in such practices over time, there will naturally follow a dating of the expression—to the point that it is no longer usable. Think about it...

Land of Milk and Honey

In a time gone by, this used to mean a place which offered delightful food potential. But do the two food items cited, "milk and honey", still exemplify a typical preferred diet, in modern times—in light of healthier contemporary food preferences?

Even if "milk" and "honey" are to be retained, in some form, in the use of this expression, they need to be replaced with healthier choices, such as in, "The land of 2%-fat milk and sugar-free honey".

But some healthy eating hard-liners would probably want us to go further than that. No doubt they'd prefer something like, "The land of fat-free yogurt and wheat germ, nothing artificial added". Just food for thought—or food to actually eat?

Good Providers

There are other expressions which, over time, have become outdated due to changing diet preferences, in favor of healthier choices.

I am referring to the actions of the person in the typical household who is primarily responsible for being the Good Provider. You know which actions I mean: to "Put bread on the table" and "Bring home the bacon".

Time for these old expression warhorses to give way to alternatives more acceptable to modern, healthy-eating English users. I'll go with: "Put broccoli on the table", and "Bring home the high omega-fatty-acid fish".

Just so we're clear, Detective Sergeant: the "fish" part of "fish and chips" would probably satisfy my second proposed maxim—if you agree to ditch the "chips". And Hong Kong Banker: if the Chinese food in

Hong Kong is similar enough to the Chinese food in New York, then your "shrimp and broccoli" would easily satisfy both.

Salty Language

Shame on anyone who advises someone to "take it with a grain of salt" without first ascertaining whether the person you are speaking to suffers from hypertension, also known as high blood pressure. Given what we've learned in recent years of how salt intake can raise blood pressure.

I'll bet most users of this expression haven't even bothered to first find out, how much is a "grain" of salt, anyway? How many milligrams are in one grain?

If you are behooved to make use of this expression, because nothing else will suffice, could you at least go with "Take it with a *milligram* of salt", until and unless you determine the blood pressure of the listener, so that more than a milligram could still be in the safe range?

Judge, L.A. Playwright, and Hong Kong Banker: as the most senior of our advanced copy recipients, surely you would all appreciate cautious use of this expression? Of course we'd all like to see a reduction in the frequency of strokes and heart attacks brought about by hypertension.

Hot Hotcakes

Maybe there was a time when "hotcakes"—a.k.a. "pancakes"—sold briskly at venues like church socials, giving birth to "Selling like hotcakes". But today? What church socials are current users of this maxim attending?

Practically everyone living *today* can and would name a food type which is a particular favorite of theirs and which they would anoint as the epitome of popular-selling food—more deserving than "hotcakes". Some might suggest pepperoni pizza… some might choose pistachio ice cream… others might go with Drake's coffee cake…

Me? You're not gonna like this, Melbourne Sheep-Herder's Wife, but on this eater's taster, nothing beats lamb on a skewer…

Bone Appetit

"A bone to pick"… "A bone of contention"… "Make no bones about it"… All three of these frequently used expressions relate back to a truly ancient time when people actually *fought* over the last remnants of edible meat attached to a bone of a killed animal being consumed.

While we still do eat food off of a bone, we are now (presumably) too "civilized" to actually fight with each other over the remaining attached morsels. There's usually nothing to fight over, anyway: we are served our own separate portion, and what's left to consume on a bone is entirely ours, to eat or not to eat, except for what we choose to share with a significant other (with whom there will be no bone to pick, or bone of contention—and will make no bones about it.)

Since contemporary food eating customs no longer comport with the customs those three valued expressions were derived from, should we discontinue their use? Eventually, perhaps—but not until suitable substitutes have been developed. These three are too widely used, to good effect. Abruptly going cold turkey on these maxims would be... a bonehead move.

MODERNER TIMES

Riotous Act

It never ceases to amaze me how many English speakers continue to routinely say, "I read [past tense] [someone] the Riot Act," to suggest that they are getting ultimately strict with that person—without having even the foggiest notion about the actual Riot Act: when and where it was enacted and what it prohibits. (Be honest, Judge, with all your knowledge of THE LAW—do you even know?)

Here are the key facts, according to Wikipedia [and don't say, dear readers, that I never imparted to you any actual useful information]: The Riot Act was enacted by the British Parliament in 1714 and 1715 and said that local authorities could declare that any assembly of 12 or more persons was unlawful and forced to disperse.

So I say now, more than 300 years later, that if any of you are contemplating use of this expression, DO NOT do so, UNLESS you are trying to prevent the assembly of 12 or more persons. Say something else.

If you just want to indicate that you got tough with someone, what's wrong with simply saying, "I read [past tense] [that person] the Second Amendment"? Won't that get your point across?

[Warning: my suggesting the linguistic utility of such an expression should in no way be construed as a *political* endorsement of gun rights.]

Cats, Dogs and Rain

I believe I really did read this once, somewhere on the web, though I can't remember where: in medieval times, people kept their pet cats and dogs up on the roof, so that when it rained heavily, the cats and dogs would slide off. Hence the derivation of "It's raining cats and dogs," an expression suggesting exceptionally heavy rainfall.

This expression must be replaced, if not outlawed altogether. Bad enough that almost no one who uses it understands what heavy rain has to do with "cats and dogs", but worse, the derivation apparently stems from a practice, in older, less enlightened times, in which our most beloved mammal pets, cats and dogs, were abusively kept on roofs, subjecting them to the danger of falling off in times of heavy rain. We should hardly be, in effect, in this day and age, still celebrating this barbaric practice by continuing to use a language expression derived from it.

Far be it from me to practically demand the cancellation of an expression without already having come up with suitable replacements. I believe I have. Consider:

+ It's raining backed up sewers
+ It's raining wet lower pant legs
+ It's raining umbrellas turned inside out

Hey, BBBBB, perhaps you can honor us with your choice here, since rain destroys your favorite—and possibly only—reading time.

Druthers

If I had my WHAT? My *druthers*? I make use of "If I had my druthers" all the time, yet I am behooved to inquire: What the Hell *is* a "druther"? And while I'm in this inquisitive mode, why are we always seeking more than one of them?

I did go on to research this matter on the internet—which, as the author of this book, I suppose I am obliged to do. And guess what: it's not a "thing" to begin with. It's a contraction of what began, in English, as "would rather". In effect, what began linguistic eons ago, as "If I could do what I'd rather do", somehow morphed, with fits and starts, into "If I had my druthers".

Many of you are probably asking at this point: so what's the big deal? There are lots of expressions where the user doesn't actually know the derivation but knows what the overall expression means from long-term absorption of it—both hearing and using. Like "raining cats and dogs". And unlike the latter expression, "had my druthers" has no political baggage.

But it does have baggage of a different sort: the word "druthers" has *no other use whatsoever* in the English language except as a component of this expression. Imagine the frustration of an English learner who encounters "If I had my druthers" for the first time and has absolutely no idea, from any prior familiarity, what the key word "druther" refers to? Not to mention more than one of them? So I ask: is it practicable—or fair—to ask English learners to tackle this word just to use it in this one expression?

I say *no*—as long as there are viable alternatives to "If I had my druthers". And there are. Such as: "If I had my way", or "If I had my preference".

I concede there's no urgent need to cancel this expression; but it does make sense to phase it out over time to improve the English language and make it more learner-friendly.

Pennies and Pounds

I feel like I have to keep reminding people that we, Americans, *won* that little contretemps with Britain, more or less culminating in the surrender of Cornwallis at Yorktown in 1780-whenever. Because once again, I am reminded that we talk like we *lost*—as in the persistent use of "pennywise and pound foolish". In which the "pound" refers to the British monetary unit!

It's a perfectly good expression, in its intended meaning—that being too focused on saving on small costs could cause you to lose even greater amounts later on. And it's pretty obvious that when the expression first came into use, it was pre-1780-whenever, and we still were using pounds as a monetary unit!

But hey, fellow U.S. citizens, hundreds of years have passed. Don't you think that by now we could have abandoned the reference in this maxim to the British pound and substituted one for a good old American money unit — as in, "pennywise and dollar foolish", or—my favorite—"pennywise and buck foolish"? (Which better comports with "passing the buck" and "the buck stops here".)

This is no minor matter. The expression has the potential to teach a valuable lesson in economics. Yet many children growing up here, when hearing this expression, just won't get it, because when they hear "pound" they won't think it's a reference to a monetary unit greater than the penny, or any monetary unit, for that matter; instead, they'll think of some measure of *weight*—not money. The opportunity for a lesson in sound money management will be lost.

This linguistic gaffe is for the U.S. Congress to resolve—not my proposed EWL—since this is purely a U.S.A. problem; in the U.K. they still use pounds, of course.

In fact, it might even make sense for the expression to be retained in the U.S., for use only in the rare circumstance when a U.K. company has an American subsidiary. It would make sense for such a company to be careful—but not *too* careful—how it spends money in the U.S. ("pennies") because of how it will ultimately affect profits, as reflected in the books in the U.K. ("pounds").

Hong Kong Banker: this whole topic is right up your alley. Not only professionally, but personally. I assume that the British pound is no longer used as a medium of exchange in Hong Kong. Nor is the British penny. So here's a good test for your young wife: spring "pennywise and pound foolish" on her, in English, and see if she can make any sense of it.

SECTION 7—GOING BOTH WAYS

It's not about what you probably think, Detective Sergeant.
   It's about *having* it both ways—or trying to. In so many words...

DOGGING IT

"Works like a dog" vs. "A dog's life": Which is it? Can't be both. Either dogs (or most, as we've seen, above) work very hard to earn their keep, *or* they are all just lazy sons (and daughters) of bitches, without a care in the world. As suggested by "A dog's life". Pick one.
   Just curious, Melbourne Sheep-Herder's Wife: where do sheep fit in, in this bifurcated vision of the life of a domesticated mammal: are their lives closer to "Works like a sheep" or "It's a sheep's life"?

WORD ORDER

A highly esteemed expert on a field of study is often referred to as "The first word" on that subject. But that same expert might also be hailed as "The *final* word" on that same subject. Huh? How can this expert be *both*?
   Well, at least users of both expressions agree on one thing: it's not prestigious to be lumped somewhere in the middle.

CARDIOLOGICAL

"Heart of gold", which means a caring, generous heart, vs. "Hard-hearted", which means quite the opposite. I'm not a metallurgist, but isn't gold a pretty "hard" metal, as metals go? So that these two expressions are incompatible? Can't resist: together they're a bloody hard sell?
   How about, instead of "Heart of gold", using "Heart of lithium"? This metal's fairly valuable nowadays, too, yet a helluva lot lighter.

ORAL FIXATION

It's not about what you probably think, Detective Sergeant.

As you *should* have figured, knowing what this book is all about, Detective Sergeant, it's about *word*s going in and out of mouths, as in: "You're putting words in my mouth" and "You took the words right out of my mouth."

The first pertains to "bad" words you don't agree with, which someone is wrongly implying you said; while the second pertains to "good" words you do agree with, which someone preemptively says before you can—perhaps usurping your glory.

These two expressions are not necessarily inconsistent; they can co-exist in regular usage. But one has to wonder why the usage opportunities here are not broadened. For example, why don't people ever put "good" words in our mouths, implying that we said something worthy, although we didn't actually say it yet? Or, why don't we ever say that someone took the "bad" words right out of our mouth, humbly admitting that what someone already said, amounting to "misinformation", was something we were *about* to say? Thus saving us from embarrassment?

Do think about it, Sheep-Herder's Wife. At the very least, reading—and rereading—this passage might help you fall asleep. As an alternative to ... counting real sheep. Or did I just take words out of your mouth?

MORE OR LESS

Sure the whole is often "greater than the sum of its parts." But how about the opposite phenomenon, where more turns out to be *less*? As in: "Too many cooks spoil the broth"?

SECTION 8—NOW OR NEVER

Many expressions suggest happenings that in fact have *never* happened in all of human history—and likely never will. Yet we keep on using these fantasy maxims.

Does this make sense? Shouldn't every expression in use have *some* basis in reality? At least a possibility of having occurred?

Oh, I can hear some of you: you think this so-called "problem" is too rare to amount to much more than a tempest in a teapot. [That's one of them.] Rare? Really? Doubters consider, for usage expunction, on the grounds of historical impossibility, all of the following …

SH*T HIT

It did? The *fan*? Really? WHEN?? I challenge any of you readers who have ever used "The sh*t hit the fan" to document a single, actual occurrence of the action described.

As for me, it's practically impossible to prove a negative. So let's look at the proposed happening logically.

If the fan in question was a ceiling fan, already turned on, and it was your intention to get the fan to spew around a certain quantity of sh*t, how would you go about accomplishing that feat? Throwing the stuff up at the fan, from the floor, hoping it would arrive at the intended location, so that it would then be distributed as planned? Such accurate tossing would require the arm skills of no less than an Aaron Rogers or Tom Brady—rare personages in terms of the required athletic skills, and who knows if either of these gentlemen has any interest in participating in such an experiment.

Wait—you say—what about making use of a stool (no pun intended) which you place under the turned on fan so that you could get on top of the stool with the stuff in your hand, thus facilitating far more accurate placement? Really! Is that a serious suggestion? Even assuming the required accuracy could be attained, who in their right mind—and nose—would ever attempt such a challenge?

Okay—you say—forget the ceiling fan. How about a standing fan or one sitting on a table? Accurate positioning could then be achieved fairly easily, you'd think. But that's not the end of it. We'd still be left with the inevitable impossibility of the event due to the certain denial of permission from the owner of the premises. If it's someone other than you, why on earth would that person ever consent to such a widespread soiling; and if it's you, why would you consent to such a soiling of your own premises, sharply reducing the quality of life for anyone living there (not to mention what you could rent it for.) Especially when there are so many other—cleaner—options available to create a chaotic condition. If that (presumably) was your goal all along.

If anyone tells you that he or she actually witnessed such an event, you can tell that person that the author of *Damn English!* believes that he or she is full of … it.

SHOULDER CHIPS

Okay, I get it. I suppose it *is* possible to somehow, physically, end up with a "chip"—a small piece of wood—on your shoulder. But to actually *walk around* with it on your shoulder? Without it falling off after, at most, a few seconds? And all this for what? You put it there as a dare to anyone to knock it off? Because you're bothered by something that happened to you and now you're angry at the world?

If you actually believe that someone once put a chip on his shoulder (no "his or her" here; no woman would be that stubbornly confrontational), and walked around with it, for an extended time, daring someone to knock it off, then I have a bridge I want to sell you. (Well, to be consistent with the point of this passage, I must concede that to my knowledge no one ever even tried to sell the Brooklyn Bridge to someone — let alone succeeded at it.)

BABES AND BATHWATER

Did it actually ever happen that some careless shmuck "threw out the baby with the bathwater"? Even once? Someone threw out the baby's bathwater and somehow didn't notice that the baby was still in it? Maybe, if the bather was legally blind—but then why would a responsible adult parent let another adult, with that disqualifying disability, do the bathing in the first place—let alone the later water throwing?

Sorry, this one utterly fails the could-it-ever-have-happened test. If you're reluctant to stop using it, because it fills a vital usage niche, consider an alternative for "undesirable and unintended collateral consequences". Like "killing the goose that lays the golden egg", which never actually happened either, but gets a realism pass—since it's an allusion to a happening in fiction. Or "shooting yourself in the foot", which I'll bet has actually happened—but some may shrink from using due to the gun reference. Or a "cure worse than the disease", which *has* happened many times—*too* many, as corroborated by the tsunami of malpractice lawsuits.

BULL BULL

Before you go comparing someone to a "bull in a china shop"—meaning that that person is prone to untamed, unpredictable behavior which is likely to lead to widespread indiscriminate destruction—how about first documenting a single instance when a bull actually has gained entry into a china shop, and wreaked havoc therein, as opposed to simply exiting through the front door?

DOG GONE

Card-carrying Cynics love to observe, "It's a dog-eat-dog world." Really? Would one of you smug Cynics please tell me when, if ever, in all of human/dog history, has a dog (a true domesticated dog, mind you, not a wolf) actually eaten another dog? Not in Korea? (Where, admittedly, it's quite possible, dog meat has made it into dog food?) [If you're reading this, it means you are not reading the Korean edition.]

THINKING CAPS

What's that? I'm supposed to put on WHAT? To do WHAT?? A THINKING cap???

I categorically state that in all my decades on this planet, at all times acutely aware of all that is happening around me, I absolutely never heard of, let alone saw, anyone wear on their head an item of attire designed to improve their intelligence, or which even serendipitously had that effect.

The very idea of a "thinking cap" is totally undermined by pragmatic considerations. Where, for example, would you buy such a cap? What would it cost? Would they come in different colors—so you could color-coordinate with the rest of your clothing? (A not insignificant consideration, according to my girlfriend, who looks over my shoulder as I write this.) Do some come with thick linings, so you could wear one outside in the cold weather? (I'd hate it if the intelligence of ski instructors was in any way compromised while they try to impart to you the dangers of avalanches and frostbite.) Might such a cap be patented—thus preventing you from making your own?

Seriously—which is, actually, how I've been proceeding all along—the idea of a "thinking *cap*" doesn't even comport with modern feminist dogma on the manner in which most men carry out the thinking process. According to those learned theorists, if men were to wear a proximate item of attire to enhance their thinking abilities, it would be a "thinking *jockstrap*".

On the other hand, I am willing to concede that an item of attire on your head could have the *opposite* effect—of *dumbing you down*. I strongly suspect that whoever came up with the concept of a "thinking cap" was, at the time, wearing a baseball cap—backwards.

A*S OR ELBOW?

While we're on the subject of human intelligence, let us scrutinize the viability of an expression that purports to epitomize human stupidity: has it ever happened, even once in all of human experience, that a human being has been unable to distinguish between two of his starkly different body parts: his own a*s and elbow? Assuming his key senses of sight and touch are in good working order? (And even without them, couldn't a reliable distinction probably be nonetheless made, depending on the timing, just by employing the senses of sound and smell?)

STRAWS AND BACKS

I ask you readers—well, the fair-minded ones, anyway: in all of humans' history with animals—in particular large mammalian beasts of burden always carrying around loads of stuff for us—did it ever happen, *even once*, that a single straw, placed on the back of such an animal, caused that back to break? In other words—as if you didn't know—I am asking whether there is any basis in reality whatsoever for the old adage, "The straw that broke the camel's back."

You know where I stand on this issue, of course—given that I state in the introduction to this Section, that it's about implied "happenings" that "in fact have never happened." As plain as I can put it—and even though I am no veterinarian—it's *impossible*, as a practical matter, for a single straw to break a camel's back. For sure, prior to that last catastrophic straw, there would have been stresses and strains on the poor beast, in particular on its back, so that as straw after straw was added, it would have prompted its handlers to stop adding straw, well before there was enough of it to actually break its back.

True, its handlers would be less motivated by genuine compassion than by pecuniary calculations—given the value of their investment in the beast—but no matter the reason, they would be vigilant in protecting the beast from any serious injury. No local "ASPCA" would therefore be needed, either, to ensure the animal's avoidance of the most serious repercussions of adding straw upon straw.

Now, I do appreciate that eliminating "The straw that broke the camel's back" from usage, on the ground that it lacks a basis in reality, would impose a real linguistic hardship on many English users, in that its *derivative* expression, "The last straw", is in widespread use.

But not to worry. I think there's a simple way to preserve "The last straw" by modifying the underlying expression, with the substitution of another animal for the camel—an animal whose back *could* very well break from the addition of a single straw.

Which animal? You may have already guessed: I am referring to the tiny *chihuahua*. Perhaps, as part of this language revision plan, we could train chihuahuas to carry small quantities of straw—give them an actual job to do. They are so small it's conceivable that just one added straw could unexpectedly break its back. Heck, all you need is one such occurrence to justify the evolved expression: "The straw that broke the chihuahua's back." And thereby preserve collaterally the valuable derivative "The last straw".

And into the bargain, we'd finally be putting those lazy, pampered chihuahuas to work, along with the mighty German shepherds and speedy greyhounds and all the other hard-working canines. Thus killing two birds with one stone!

KILLING TWO BIRDS WITH ONE STONE

(I know, what a serendipitous segue. Did I purposely position this section to directly follow the previous one? You need to ask?)

Did anyone ever actually kill two flying birds with one thrown stone? By throwing the stone so precisely, at the first flying bird, that it bounced off and, at the perfect flight angle, went on to hit *another* bird, flying nearby, in both instances hitting the birds so powerfully and in just the right location, that both were killed from that one throw?

This one's for the birds—or the birdbrained. If you were to tell me that you believe it could actually happen, I'd tell you that I have a bridge to sell you—if I hadn't already used that line.

Okay—to be fair—I admit that my mind is still open on the usability of this expression. But to fully change it, I'd need to see *actual video proof* of a one-stone-twin-bird-killing. If you have such a video, send it to me. Garysherbell @ gmail.com. The proof would then be in the video—if not the pudding.

Aha! Another serendipitous segue to another expression, which conveniently allows me to "kill" two expressions in one section. Pray tell: has any significant proof of anything important ever been found in *pudding*? Even in theory, I can only think of one scenario: arsenic or cyanide found in pudding consumed by the decedent, in a murder-by-poison investigation. But I don't know for a fact that any such crime discovery ever took place. Judge, Detective Sergeant, would you happen to know of one such real-life episode? Sorry, L.A. Playwright: fiction doesn't count.

SECTION 9—SENSELESS AND NONSENSICAL NONSENSE, MAKING NO SENSE AT ALL

(Needs no introduction.)

HOWDIE

Logically we begin our conversation on this topic with an expression that begins so many others, when people who never met before are introduced: "How do you do?" Now, read that again, and this time, slowly, trying to absorb what the asker is actually, literally, asking the askee to reveal. That's right, askees are apparently being asked to now explain, in some detail, how they go about doing what they usually do—most likely, for a living.

This could well produce at best confusing and at worst entirely unnecessary exchanges. For example, a doctor on the receiving end of a "How do you do?" might feel obliged to immediately respond with an "I take Medicare and Medicaid". Or a doctor who's a male gynecologist might want to defensively launch right into a "There's another woman in the examination room at all times." Or a proctologist, in a jocular mood, might go with "I do know my a*ses from my elbows." All this a waste of time before the asker has been able to clarify the nature of his or her inquiry.

How nonsensical to employ this initial meeting greeting when there is such potential for misunderstanding. How much more sense it would make to employ instead a simpler greeting, like "Pleased to meet you." But DO NOT consider substituting, in a first meeting context, with a "How are you?" Though the question makes sense on its face, it can as well, when taken literally, lead to confusion and the waste of time. Last thing you want to hear in response, after that initial "How are you?", is something like, "Well, to be honest, I am a little constipated right now."

TRUST THRUST

"I don't trust him as far as I can throw him": this one doesn't make a bit of sense, not even a smidgeon. It implies that a fellow can be trusted only as far as he can be *thrown*—not a substantial distance, generally speaking, when throwing humans, and therefore not a whole lot of trust to be had. (Note: Though the maxim traditionally refers to "hims", it could, of course, equally apply to "hers".)

To begin with: smaller, lighter people obviously can be thrown further than bigger, heavier ones. Yet there simply isn't a bit of evidence—not one iota—that there's any correlation whatsoever between a person's weight, or size, and his or her trustworthiness. Why should we believe, for example, that, say, Mickey Rooney was even a tad more trustworthy than, say, Wilt Chamberlain? Such correlative perceptions could even undermine well established historical perspectives. For example, are we now to assume that Napoleon, all along, was more to be trusted than Wellington?

But the worst of it is that there are *discriminatory* implications in this expression—*disparate impacts*—which literally shock the conscience: to the effect that certain *whole groups* of people, solely because of their *greater* size, on average, are therefore also, on average, *less* trustworthy. This heinous line of thinking—*short supremacy*—would not only apply to comparisons of people from different races and nationalities, but also to people of *different genders*. Since men, on average, are *bigger* than women, on average, are we now to conclude that, generally speaking, men are *less* to be trusted?

Just imagine, Judge, how such a biased perception might have affected your professional judgement when faced with sharply divergent "he said/she said" claims? And what unwarranted effect might it have had on your trustworthiness analysis if you were to learn that the woman appearing before you is actually a transgender biological male?

And how about you, Detective Sergeant? Surely you've had much experience on the matter of male vs. female trustworthiness—both as dater and arrester? Did size matter? (Not what you're thinking.) Care to share?

The pernicious effect of the biased implications inherent in this expression strongly suggest the need for a progressive analysis of its continued suitability. We can no longer remain complacent and look—or listen—away when faced with structural linguistic discrimination.

FLYING CROWS

"As the crow flies" means, of course, a distance measured, theoretically, point-to-point, in a perfectly straight line, as opposed to the distance a vehicle would actually have to travel, to make the same trip on imperfectly straight roads.

Pardon me for pointing this out to you satisfied frequent users of this one, but has any qualified ornithologist ever authoritatively established that crows—which are, after all, befitted with bird brains—do in fact always fly in a straight line? I mean, never get diverted, even once by, say, changing directions when espying an aggressive hawk ahead? Or get lost? Or just plain meander, while enjoying the "bird's-eye" view?

Heck—no, this time I think I'll go with Hell—I was an A-student in biology in high school, and even I can't offer an educated guess on the matter. However, I can concede that I don't know, with any degree of certainty, that crows *don't* always fly straight, either. Therefore, I will continue to use the expression until such time as I receive an authoritative answer to the question.

RISK LIFE AND ... LIMB?

Sure, no sensible person would argue that when we are engaged in some dangerous activity it's the risk to our very *life* which is our paramount concern. But what comes in *second*? The risk to a *limb*? Really? Is the risk to a limb the body part risk that is clearly in second place? MEN, I'M TALKING TO YOU.

THE DEPTH OF BEAUTY

"Beauty is only skin deep," it's said.

Now, I have no interest in—or stomach for—taking on the "Beauty-is-only-skin-deep feminist lobby", but as an honest linguistics commentator, I am behooved to point out what others have observed: that the skin does cover—what?—98 percent of the body, except for—what?—the eyeballs and the toe and fingernails, so doesn't the skin plainly make up in *breadth* for what it lacks in *depth*?

Hey, I didn't say I *agreed* with this sexist point of view—only that some *othe*r folks, hopelessly shallow ones, have said it! (Isn't it ironic that if you disagree that "beauty is only skin deep", you're tagged as "*shallow*".)

BBBBB, as a self-described "beauty", I'd—no, *we'd* all be interested in your take on this issue. Though I wonder if you could offer one, on this topic, which would be honest and humble…

…Hey, BBBBB, just pulling your leg!

(I was thinking of lampooning this very "leg pull" expression earlier, in the "never once happened" section, but passed on it. And now here I am, actually using it, just the same. Might as well go with it then: How *silly* this one is! I'm no doctor, but has anyone *ever* made someone laugh by pulling their leg? That's all there is to it. Now you see why I passed.)

[My further wry remarks—on my actually interacting with BBBBB's legs, sometime in the future—have been edited for content.]

PROBLEM PREPS

Not prep schools… but *prepositions*, so often misused in our beloved language. As in [two prepositions that are okay here, by the way]:

For Crying Out Loud

Suppose your upstairs neighbor is raucously playing his tuba. In a huff, you run upstairs, knock on the door, and when he opens it, you confront him with an irate, "For crying out loud, would you stop playing that damn tuba?"

My question: why the preposition "for" in front of "crying out loud"? Yes, you are "crying out loud"—that part is correct. But are you asking him to stop playing the tuba "for" your crying out loud? Saying in other words, that his *stopping* the tuba playing would "bring about" your crying out loud, when what has obviously happened is the very opposite?

Substituting for "for" with "via my" or "upon my" or "as per my" or "following my" or "to stop my" would all improve the accuracy of your exhortation. Yet these variations all suffer from a lack of "oomph"—not to mention vital brevity. Perhaps, fellow word-smith L.A. Playwright, you can think of a substitution which attains sufficient accuracy while retaining oomphy brevity?

For Christ's Sake
Suppose that instead of beginning with "For crying out loud" to that noisy tuba player you'd started with "For Christ's sake", continuing with, as before, "would you stop playing that damn tuba"? Frankly, I don't see how this use of "for" is any better. I'm no theologian, but I honestly fail to see how his stopping the tuba playing would somehow benefit Christ. For *my* sake, maybe—but *Christ's*?

However, if you're determined to employ fire and brimstonish religious precepts to bolster your persuasion, perhaps you can go with, "For your *own* sake—to avoid Hell—stop playing that damned tuba!"

Judge, any ideas on how an allusion to the Jewish religion could enhance your persuasion?

Can't See the Forest For the Trees
Oh sure, we all know what the originator of this expression was aiming for: to suggest that getting bogged down in scrutinizing the details—the "trees"—could well cause you to miss seeing the Big Picture—the "forest". But what's the "for" for? *For* the trees? The overall intent of the expression—and its cleverly using the tree-forest analogy—is laudable, but I'm afraid the expression ultimately fails in its execution due to the misused preposition "for".

Though wordier, wouldn't it make more sense to instead say something like, "Because of excessive focus on the individual trees, you could miss appreciating the whole forest"? L.A. Playwright: hate to bother you again. But maybe you can weigh in on this one as well, with a workable substitute?

Pissed Off
Who decided on "off" instead of "on"?

It would seem that to indicate that someone is really angry, "pissed *on*" would be the way to go, given that the use of "off" suggests that the anger has ended, when in fact it's still very much in play, or at least was, just following the provocation in question. I would also point out that the act of urinating on—"pissing on"—someone is bound to upset them, further solidifying "pissed *on*" as the more logical usage choice.

Hitting It Off
This one's used to suggest that two people who have recently gotten to know each other have been getting along really well—"clicking", it's sometimes said. The expression is usually applied in a romantic context, but could be applied in other contexts as well—such as in an employer-employee relationship.

And once again, I'm linguistically—er, pissed *on*—over the use of the preposition "off" instead of the clearly more appropriate preposition "on", which far better implies that something "good" is happening, rather than something "bad". Just look, for instructive comparison, at the use of "turn off" (bad) vs. "turn on" (good). And look again at "hitting on" someone, which means an initial attraction (good); indeed, if the target responds positively, the "hitting on" could well lead to the couple—under current usage—"hitting it off". But does that switch in midstream—from a "good on" to a "good off"—make linguistic sense? (Remember, too, that earlier I came down hard on the use of "hitting on" for *political* reasons, not linguistic.) Was the originator of "hitting it off" possibly "off" the wagon (not sober—bad) vs. "on" the wagon (sober—good) at the time of creation?

Into the bargain, "hitting it off" would make perfect sense if it meant the *bad* opposite of what it does now: a couple breaking up, as in a divorce. But "hitting it off" has already been inexplicably "taken", for the "good" usage.

Alas, the originator settled on "hitting it off" way too quickly, probably without giving it much thought, and we are, to this day, stuck with his (probably a man's) choice. Since then, we've all simply followed the linguistic choice he made—like sheep. (Sorry if that offends you, Melbourne Sheep-Herder's Wife.)

Ups and Downs
What linguistic genius first came up with the idea to put the preposition "up" after the verb "screw" or "screwed", or "mess" or "messed", or some other common verbs I can think of? Instead of the preposition "down", which, directionwise, is far more consistent with the pejorative connotations implied? Given that "up" is almost universally applied in positive contexts, such as in "uplifting", or "things are looking up"?

Okay, I can hear some of you cynical nitpickers right now saying, Oh yeah? What about "Up yours"? What's so "uplifting" about that exclamation (at least, in the emotional sense, as opposed to the purely physical sense?)

My response is that "Up yours" *can* be quite *up*lifting, even emotionally, to the *speaker* of those words. Who is ferociously getting back at the targeted hostile listener.

TOPSY-TURVY

You've heard it said dozens of times before: that someone, say, a guy, who is joyously in love with some gal, is "head over heels" in love with her.

Well, users of that expression, sorry to puncture your linguistic romantic bubble, but that expression makes absolutely no sense, from the anatomical perspective. 99 percent of the time, our heads are either over our heels, when we are standing or sitting, or at least on the same level as our heels, when we are lying down. Just about the only time our heels are above our heads is when we are doing something acrobatic, like *cartwheels*—which is precisely the demonstration of exuberance the "head over heels" expression is alluding to.

That expression therefore has it all backwards—er, upside down. To be anatomically correct, when describing the madly in love cartwheeling fellow, go with "heels over head" in love.

BEST FEET

"Putting your best foot forward" makes no sense at all—for the simple reason that no one, naturally, has one foot which is demonstrably "better" than the other.

Disagree? Let's pursue this further. Honest answer, please: which of you readers actually has one foot which is so different from the other that you could fairly say that one is "better" than the other? For putting-forward purposes? I doubt not many—maybe *not even one*.

Here's my offer: take photos of your two feet and email them to me (garysherbell @ gmail.com.) If I honestly think that one of your feet is clearly "better" than the other I'll send you a special, signed commendation to that effect. [Disclaimer: the foot difference can't be due to some trauma—like an accident which required full or partial amputation, or otherwise resulted in horrible disfigurement. Nor can it be the result of some disease, like gangrene, diabetes or leprosy. Also—remember—it's not enough to have ugly toes; you'd need to demonstrate toes which are, naturally, far uglier on one foot than on the other.]

STEP WATCH

On the subject of forward-moving feet…

Perhaps the dumbest advice ever promoted in an English expression can be found in "Watch your step". Think about it: if you follow that advice, and look down at your feet while you walk, you are almost certain to bump into something ahead you didn't see in time.

ONE AND DONE

Why just one?

Put Your Feet Down
Meaning: to emphasize your opposition, your refusal to go along. But why limit your visual emphasis to putting down just *one* foot? Why not—when applicable—better demonstrate your adamant opposition by putting *both* feet down? By, say, jumping up and landing on both feet?

Feet Fetish
Why is it that when a man (usually a man) has a peculiar sexual obsession with women's feet, it's invariably referred to as a "foot" fetish, when for sure the fellow is equally obsessed with *both* feet of a target female? Just curious, mind you, as a totally non-participating observer. (Merely liking women in three-inch stiletto heels doesn't count, right?)

You can help me out here, BBBBB. Wouldn't you agree that when a man approaches you on a beach, and appears to focus on your feet, he always spends equal time (ogling, massage offering) on *both*, as opposed to just one?

Handy
Why do people who ask for your assistance always ask you to "lend *a* hand", instead of *both* hands? As in "Lend me your hands?" Is it some ego thing? Pride? The asker doesn't want to admit that he or she needs *double* the assistance, from two hands, that he would get from one?

Handsmade
Why is something made by hand always described as "*hand*made", implying made by people using one hand, instead of "*hands*made", that is, made by people using *both* hands?

When looking for an explanation, and are still unsure, I always say, fall back on "follow the money". Could it be that by saying that an item for sale is "*hand*made", that is, made by a person using one hand, it implies it took twice as long to make as the same item made by someone using *two* hands—thus justifying double the price?

Hong Kong Banker: you know a thing or two about economics. Does this explanation make sense to you? (I'm sure you'd have no *political* problem with agreeing; any criticism of greedy capitalism would probably sit quite well with your government. In any case I assure you, your reply will be strictly confidential.)

<u>Eye Eye</u>

I concede that it makes little difference whether you and another person "see eye to eye" or, using both eyes, "see eyes to eyes". Mean pretty much the same thing. Ditto for "Giving someone the eye" or "Keeping an eye on someone"; using both eyes to do the job would probably not significantly add to the likelihood of success.

Not so, though, with "There's more here than meets the eye". For sure, one might legitimately point out, to a user, "Well, duh, maybe you'd have seen *more* if you'd used *both* eyes." The upshot: If you did use both eyes, say so—"There's more than meets the *eyes*." It would then at least be clear that you did employ maximum visual scrutiny.

PLACES IN THE HEART

No doubt you've heard "It warms the cockles of my heart". Only one problem with that old maxim: there ain't no "cockles" in them there hearts.

Ditto for the "heartstrings" one supposedly might pull or tug.

There is, however, a "bottom of the heart", as in, "I thank you from the bottom of my heart"—words of deeply felt gratitude or sympathy. On the other hand, there's a more anatomically correct name for the bottom of the heart: the ventricles.

In the interests of cardio correctness, I propose:

+ Ditch "cockles"
+ Ditch "heart strings"
+ Switch from "bottom" to "ventricles"

Agree with me here and you get my heartfelt thanks.

BUTTER UP

"Knowing which side your bread is buttered on" has long mystified me. Not its meaning—knowing how to get ahead by pleasing someone in power (a.k.a. knowing whose a*s to kiss)—but its *derivation*. That is: what the Hell it has to do with buttering bread. Otherwise put: what does buttering your bread on a particular side have to do with self advancement?

But before I get further into this topic, it has just occurred to me that it probably doesn't even belong in this section. Since it pertains to cholesterol-high "butter" and "bread" (not necessarily lower-carb whole wheat bread) it probably better pertains to the previously covered topic of "old food expressions" now in need of revision due to modern healthier diet prescriptions. Perhaps it should be moved there. To be discussed with my editor.

WHERE YOU WEAR

Yes, it's *that* body part, again, the one which more often pops up in English expressions than any other (not what you're thinking, Detective Sergeant.) I'm talking about the *heart*, and this time it's employed in "Wearing your heart on your sleeve".

If your usage objective here is to point out that someone speaking is showing his or her emotions outwardly, for all to see, then the "sleeve" location is way too far from the speaker's head to effectively make the point. Not even close. When you look at someone who's speaking to you, how often, if ever, do you look away from the speaker's head, and down at that person's *sleeve*? Rarely. How can we therefore expect someone new to English, someone struggling to learn it, to get the import of this maxim, given how far away the speaker's sleeves are from his or her head? Would be almost as bad as saying, "Wearing his heart on his knee pads".

To better make the point you ought to refer to a different clothing location—one closer to the head. For example: "He wears his heart on his collar". Or dispense with a clothing reference altogether and go with "He wears his heart around his neck".

Okay, conceded: there might be an occasion when it's appropriate to place the speaker's heart, in this expression, at a distant location. For example, if a fellow is truly in love with the woman he's being intimate with, you might legitimately want to go with, "He's wearing his heart on his—". You can fill in the rest, Detective Sergeant.

UPSIDE DOWN

I'm no theologian, but... when something stinks alot, I mean, *really* alot, shouldn't we be saying it "Stinks to low Hell", not "Stinks to High Heaven"? [Just had to include this in a book titled "*Damn* English!"]

POWER COUPLE

Continuing with the theological theme...

What deep thinker came up with the names for our most illustrious Power Couple: Father Time and Mother Nature? For it's as plain as Newton's falling apple that the Couples' essential skills, reflected in their sobriquets, should be switched. "*Father* Nature" and "*Mother* Time" far better comport with reality—at least, *my* reality, when growing up.

It was my mother, not my father, who was in charge of time. It was *she* who said to me in the morning, five days a week, "Get up! Time for school!" And it was *she* who said to me every day, when I was playing outside (except Sundays, when we went out for Chinese food), "Come in! Time for dinner!" It was my father, on the other hand, as the primary wage earner, who determined the very *nature* of our existence: where we could afford to live, where we could afford to go on vacation, and how often we could go out for Chinese food.

ON TIME

I'm just getting warmed up on the subject of time. Time and again, the concept of "time" presents fertile ground for nonsensicals which fail to verbally give us the right time. No time, of course, to present all of them, so here and now—no time like the present—are just some of the worst language offenders:

Tail Shakes
Among the many ways to describe a very short time are "in a heartbeat", or the even faster "blink of an eye", or the extremely fast "in a flash". And then there's the moderately slower, but still considerably fast "two shakes of a lamb's tail". Which brings us to the curiously missing from usage "*one* shake of a lamb's tail". Since one shake of a lamb's tail is presumably *twice* as fast as two shakes, why is there no history of using it, especially when looking for an alternative to the other ultrafast expressions? Melbourne Sheep-Herder's Wife: can you help me here? Do you know why "one shake of a lamb's tail" never made it into usage to describe something especially quick?

Untimely
And then there's "in no time at all" and "immediately if not sooner": they both appear to suggest a passage of time even faster than the ones noted above—indeed they imply that *zero time* has or will be passed while something has happened or will be happening. But that makes no sense at all. Both are clearly incompatible with the laws of physics, up to and

including Einstein's Theory of Relativity. Which I read last night. To write this passage. Okay, skimmed. For all of—one shake of a lamb's tail.

INSANITRYING

Yes, ol'Albert famously devised his revered Theory of Relativity, but perhaps even more valuable for humanity, at least for everyday employment, is the definition of "insanity" he reportedly came up with: doing the same thing over and over, each time expecting a different result. But doesn't this pearl of accepted wisdom in turn make nonsensical many heretofore hallowed advisory expressions? Like: "If at first you don't succeed, try, try again"? Which "insanely" urges us to keep on making the same efforts to succeed even though they so far have miserably failed us each and every time?

To reconcile these conflicting advisories, perhaps we need to recognize some "Sanity Limit": the number of duplicate failed efforts you are permitted before attempting yet another one marks you as "insane"? Which number depends on the context and therefore is all … relative?

BEDSIDE MANNER

"Got up on the wrong side of the bed?" That one's often asked of someone who appears to be acting "out of sorts". But it seems to this language observer that it's the *asker* of that nonsensical question who has some 'splaining to do. For *even if* the askee has an actual choice of which side of the bed to get up on in the morning, and *even if* there would be a theoretical "wrong side" for the askee to get up on, how on earth would getting up on this so-called "wrong side" throw the askee into some kind of mood tizzy? What would be the causal connection?

Wouldn't it therefore make more sense to instead ask whether something had happened *while* getting out of bed which actually *could* result in a foul temperament? Like: "Step on a thumbtack getting out of bed, and realized it's been decades since your last tetanus shot?" OR, "While getting out of your lower bunk, hit your head on the upper bunk bed?" OR, "When you got out of bed, discover that the person you spent the night with left without saying a word?" All of these questions would stand a much better chance of uncovering the askee's real reason for appearing "out of sorts". (An expression which—by the way—could use some scrutiny of its own. Later, perhaps.)

DOGCATCHER ELECTIONS

You've heard it so many times before: He (or she) "couldn't get elected dogcatcher!" A derisive reference to someone whose elective prospects are so minimal that that person couldn't even get elected to the elective office supposedly bottom-of-the-barrel easiest to get elected to.

Another expression with commendable intentions which nonetheless fails—in the execution. For the simple reason that to my knowledge, the office of "Dogcatcher" is nowhere in these United States an elective office—if it ever was. It would be a grave mistake to continue to perpetuate this myth of dogcatcher elections—as implied by this expression—especially in this day and age when so many are vitriolically opposed to any political "misinformation".

Of course, it's one thing to demand the cancellation of an expression, and quite another to come up with a workable substitute. But I think I have. Instead of "dogcatcher" we should be referring to the mayor of the smallest town in the state of the United States with the smallest population. Now let's see which that is... Going to the web...

... Aha! Got it. Okay, from now on, if you want to refer to someone's pathetic inelectability, please say, instead, he (or she) "couldn't get elected mayor of Lost Springs, Wyoming."

BEAN HILLS

Don't get me wrong. Humphrey Bogart is my favorite actor of all time. And *Casablanca* is among my three or four favorite *film*s of all time. Yet, I am behooved to report, that when, at the end of that movie, in the famous airport finale, Bogie says to Ingrid Bergman, "The problems of three little people don't amount to a *hill of beans* in this world", he misses the expression boat in utterly failing to appreciate the actual value of a typical "hill of beans". He implies that the value of such a quantity of beans is quite small, when in fact, it's value is potentially *enormous*.

Here's looking at you, beans—on the web. After I researched it I was *shocked! shocked!* that he could be so wrong. It turned out that green beans are currently selling at $3.15 per pound. So do the math (and check this out, Hong Kong Banker): An entire hill of beans—remember, we're not talking about a pile, but a whole *hill*—has to have at least a ton of beans, which means 2,000 pounds per ton. Multiply 2,000 by 3.15 and you get a total bean value of over $6,000!

Sorry, Bogie, there's real value in them thar bean hills. Don't say it again—and think of some other way to say to Ingie that the "problems of three little people" don't amount to much. Why not round up the usual suspects and take a cue from Claude Rains: say they don't amount to "a bottle of Vichy water"?

Back me up on the math, Hong Kong Banker—and this could be the start of a beautiful friendship.

GIVE AND TAKE

[ANOTHER WARNING: Some material in the passage below could be considered *scatological*. Therefore, please do skip this passage if you feel that such material is beneath you. Unless, of course, at this very moment, such material is beneath you.]

Most linguistic scholars would probably agree that it makes no sense at all to say "take a crap (or sh*t)" as a stand-in (or sit-in, as it were) for defecation. After all, you are not in the act of "taking" *anything whatsoever*. On the contrary, you are doing quite the opposite: *giving* something, as per the applicable flow direction.

Why, then, did our English language creators go with "take" a crap (or sh*t) instead of "give"? Probably because to "give" a crap (or sh*t) was already—well, *taken*—as a way of saying "*caring* about something". (Which usage actually makes sense: when you really care about something, it tends to unnerve you, loosening the contents of your lower bowel—hence leading to the very reasonable derivative verb phrase, "to give a crap (sh*t)".)

Not that "taking a crap (sh*t)" is an utterly defenseless linguistic choice. There's a possible method to this English madness. I can imagine that in the old-old-*old* days, when people shared the same latrine, you simply had to "take your turn"—hence the semi-reasonable gravitation toward "taking" a crap (sh*t).

Still, I believe that the initial use of "take a crap (or sh*t)" was—as you'd say, Judge—"wrongly decided", and should now be reversed. It should now be mandated that "to give a crap (sh*t)" means *to defecate*.

But, you rightly say, how then to indicate "caring" if "to give a crap (sh*t)" is no longer available? No problem. For extreme instances of *not* caring we could still employ "not giving a rat's a*s" or "not giving a flying f*ck" (as previously evaluated in this book.) For cases of less intense non-caring we could fall back on the tried and true, albeit decidedly bland, "I couldn't care less". For expressing either caring or non-caring, we could also go with the more oomphy "give (or don't give) a damn", or "give (or don't give) a f*ck" (minus the super-oomphy "flying".)

[Sheer etymological digression: The derivative use of "give a f*ck" to mean "caring" actually makes complete sense, if you think about it. Back in the language-formulation days, many people—in particular, women—only agreed to have sexual relations with people they "cared" about. It was therefore quite natural, linguistically-speaking, for "giving a f*ck" to, over the centuries, morph into a variant for "caring" in general, even when not accompanied by sexual relations.]

I do recognize what an uphill battle it would be for me to get "give a crap (sh*t)" to mean what "take a crap (sh*t)" now means. I'd be going up against hundreds of years of language precedent. And in language, there is the same stubborn adherence to precedent, Judge, that you in the legal profession call "stare decisis"—"let the decision stand". Now, in this context, one could say, "let the usage stand."

In fact, it would be such a tough fight ahead for reform that I'm on the verge of throwing in the linguistic reform towel here—and on this one issue no longer giving a damn. Or crap. Or sh*t. Or f*ck.

THE "THE"

But I still do care, and am bothered no end by, an apparently pointless "the". However, I'm not talking about the "the" in front of "Bronx", which is apparently pointless since the other four New York City boroughs—Brooklyn, Queens, Manhattan and Staten Island—do *not* have a "the" in front.

Yes, that "the", before "Bronx"—for which no adequate explanation has ever been given—is indeed pointless. But it's not my point. My point—now—is the *"the" in front of "f*ck"*, to form the phrase *"the f*ck"*, widely used for super emphasis. It's a close cousin of "f*cking" and "bloody", albeit without their grammatical contexts. Those emphasizers are most often used as adjectives ("get your f*cking/bloody hands off me"), or as adverbs ("f*cking/bloody get your hands off me")—but "the f*ck", when used for emphasis, has no apparent grammatical status. It's emphasis and nothing but emphasis—with, like the others, no connection at all per say, to the sex act.

As in various questions:

"What the f*ck do you want?"
"Why the f*ck are you here?"
"Who the f*ck do you think you are?"
"Where the f*ck are you going?"
Or in reference to a question:
"I want to know what the f*ck you want."
"Tell me why the f*ck you're here."
"So that's who the f*ck you think you are."
"Thanks for telling me where the f*ck you're going."
Or in such world-famous commands as:
"Get the f*ck outta here."
And: "Shut the f*ck up."

A side issue of some interest is why our English Creators settled on the article "the" instead of the article "a"? Did they envision that a focus on a particular "f*ck", as opposed to a more generalized reference, would better project emphasis? Am I giving these Creators too much credit for Intelligent Language Design—when in fact it was probably all decided with a coin flip? I leave that for true linguistic scholars to explore further.

My purpose here is only to expose an English nonsensical, and when appropriate, recommend an improvement. Which might, if nothing else, mean merely eliminating an unnecessary word, thereby making both written and spoken English proceed more expeditiously.

My reform proposal is actually quite simple: to dispense with the "the" in front of "f*ck", in the phrase "the f*ck", when used for emphasis.

For example: "Get the f*ck outta here" becomes "Get f*ck outta here." See, shorter, with no resulting confusion.

And "Who the f*ck do you think you are" becomes "Who f*ck do you think you are." See, again, shorter, without any confusion.

And "What the f*ck do you want" becomes "What f*ck do you…"

... Oops... Hmmm... Now that I think of it, that "the" can sometimes come in right handy. Might even be indispensable. In answer to "What f*ck do you want," last thing you want to hear is "Missionary position."

WHAT THE F*CK

... Which sex act position option conveniently provides a smooth segue to our next topic, the nonsensical description of the act as "making love"—that is, when it's used to describe the Real Thing, not used merely for emphasis. (Don't get me wrong, sexual freedom advocates: I'm not saying that the sex act is nonsensical, only that it's nonsensical to describe it as "making love".)

The phrase "making love" is commendable for its public-spirited attempt to offer a "polite" alternative to the crude Anglo-Saxon "f*ck", or to the clinical "had sex with", or to the slang variations like "screwed" or "banged". Only one problem with its usage, but it's a biggie: IT DOESN'T COMPORT WITH REALITY. For reasons as follows:

(1) Only a tiny portion of couples engaging in The Act are actually "in love" at the start of it.

(2) If they happen to be *already* in love, then the Act of engaging in sex will not be "making" any love that didn't already exist.

(3) If they are *not* already in love, at the start, it's highly unlikely that when they emerge from The Act, minutes later, they will find themselves in that serene emotional state that didn't previously exist. (Okay, male prowess boasters, if you insist: emerge "a while" later.)

Here's what we *should* be saying, instead: If you're *already* in love, then you're not *making* love, you're "*showing* love". And if you're *not* already in love, you're not *making* love, you're "*faking* love".

SAY WHAT?

I admit: I mention "Not to mention..." all the time, to introduce the last in a series of examples. Probably from force of habit, *even though I acknowledge that it makes absolutely no sense* that every single time this phrase is used, the user then promptly goes on to *mention* the very thing he or she said wouldn't be mentioned!

For the life of me, I just don't get the logic of this usage. (By the way: that expression, "for the life of me", is another solid example of a misused preposition—this time, "for". I mean, if you don't quite get the reason for the usage, is your *life* really at stake?) Someone please tell me: is there some compelling reason not to use, instead, a simple "as well as" or "in addition to", or the elegantly brief "plus"? Or, if the last of your series of examples actually possesses qualities which elevate it from the run of the mill prior mentions, why not consider going with the popular "last but not least", which at least has the distinction of shedding some further light on the last entrant? On the other hand, don't even think about switching to "to say nothing of", which demonstrates—since you *are* about to "say something of"—the very same dopey do/don't inconsistency.

Many other expressions—beyond the "added mention" context—also grossly fail to communicate the user's true meaning. Take, for instance, "I'm afraid that—", as in "I'm afraid that I'm going to have to let you go." Isn't it the person on the *receiving* end, who's about to be fired, who ought to be "afraid"—not the expression user? What's *he* got to fear? And how about when someone says, "I can't wait to—", as in "I can't wait to see the expression on his face"? Pardon me for pointing this out, user, but you *have to* wait, and *are* in fact waiting, despite your claim otherwise.

Re my admitted use of "not to mention", while hypocritically criticizing its use, I have one guilty-with-an-explanation response: as the priest said, Do as I say, not as I do. Needless to say.

SUPER DUH

There are many expressions, commonly used by English speakers and writers, which appear to say *something*, but in fact say *absolutely nothing*. Not one iota. Nada. Zilch. Here are just some of these Nothing Expressions:

+ First things first
Well *of course* first things are first. Duh. If they were *second*, they wouldn't be first. Tell me something I don't know.

+ Enough is enough
Duh, when is enough *not* enough? One example, please, of when enough *wasn't?* .... Didn't think you could come up with one.

+ What's done is done
Ditto duh. And at the same time, oddly, sometimes not even accurate. Just look at a *Halloween* movie. Is what appears to have been done to Michael Myers ever actually… *done*?

+ It is what it is
I know this inanity is extremely popular right now, but *please stop using it,* immediately, UNTIL AND UNLESS YOU CAN PRODUCE A SINGLE EXAMPLE OF SOMETHING THAT IS WHAT IT ISN'T.

+ What will be will be
The future tense version of "It is what it is". And just as dopey—and duhey—in stating the obvious.

+ When you gotta go, you gotta go
If you gotta go (to the bathroom) then *of course* you gotta go—what else? (Duh.) Prominently featured in two famous movie scenes: (1) In *The Godfather,* spoken by the police captain, when Michael, in the restaurant, asks permission to go to the bathroom (wherein he obtains the gun he uses to kill the captain); and (2) In *Jurassic Park*, spoken by the scientist Ian, when, not yet aware of the approaching T-Rex, he sees the lawyer inexplicably leave the car with the two kids, headed for the bathroom.

In fact, there are so many of these Nothing Expressions in standard use that one could construct an *entire conversation* using nothing but them. For example, here's a snippet of one, wherein two persons are in dispute over an agreement, which the first speaker seeks to cancel:

"Fair is fair."
"A deal's a deal."
"If you can't, you can't."
"When I'm right, I'm right."
Enough is en—oops. Enough said.

SECTION 10—THE FUTURE IS NOW

[Technically, this Section, the 10th section of Part One, is not actually part of Part One. Rather, it operates as a kind of "bridge" between Part One and the next part, Part Two, essentially explaining how the two Parts differ from each other. Calling it "Part Two"—with what is now called "Part Two" being called "Part Three"—was briefly considered, and rejected. This section is simply too short, it was felt, to qualify on its own as a whole Part. Also briefly considered—given its "bridge" function—was the apropos "Part 1.5"—but that title, too, was ultimately rejected, as "too mathematical." Also rejected, as untimely, was including this passage in Part Two, at its beginning, as a kind of introduction to that part. Finally it was decided to simply include this passage as the final section of Part One, albeit with this disclaimer.]

Part One of this book was (or has been, if this section is still regarded as part of it) all about the English language *as it is today*. My aim was (or has been) to point out, in this part, many of its most ridiculous and nonsensical aspects, often offering recommendations for change: from modifications and substitutions, to varied usage advisories, and, in some cases, outright cancellation.

Part Two, on the other hand, is all about *the future*: how we might shape English, going forward, thereby breathing new life into the Grand Old Language, and possibly even staving off its slow demise.

And so you will encounter in this upcoming part: not merely critiques of current words and expressions, with suggestions for change, but offerings of entirely *new* words and expressions, which in many cases fill in huge gaps in the language; proposed changes which would comport with a more progressive outlook; suggestions for improved usage which foster a more honest discourse; and my response to disturbing new language trends.

"The future is now," a famous football coach once said. Or was it Arnold Schwarzenegger in a *Terminator* movie? In any case, Arnie, in *Terminator One*, did famously say, "I'll be back." As will I, in Part Two.

To use one of my own recommendations for change in Part One: Reade on!

PART TWO—ENGLISH: WORDS IN PROGRESS

SECTION 1—A BRAVE NEW WORLD OF ENGLISH

Towards a new and improved English! (The language, not necessarily the people!) With a mouthful of brand new words and phrases to employ!

POST-MS.

Forcing women to choose between "Miss", for the unmarried, and "Mrs.", for the married, was downright discriminatory, what with men being able to go with the one status fits all "Mister" (or Mr.). Then along came the feminist pioneers, who promoted the alternative form of address of "Ms." for women—which, like "Mister", could be used by all women, regardless of their marital status.

Yet feminine-reference language reform work remains to be done. Reformers have so far "missed" out on correcting another egregious form of "missinformation": the confusion over the proper use of "Miss" vs. "Madam", or its abbreviated form "Ma'am".

"Miss" is supposed to be applied to women of a younger age, while "Madam" or "Ma'am" is intended for women of a more mature age. But how on English Earth is the user to know, in borderline cases, which is the proper term? Use "Miss" with a mature woman, and she'll likely be offended that you are not showing her due "respect"; while use of "Madam" or "Ma'am" with a young woman might devastate her ego when she isn't old enough yet, appearance-wise, to qualify for such usage. Or so she thinks: since she's never been so addressed before—in other words, she's a "ma'am virgin". (I am reminded of a *Mary Tyler Moore* show in which Mary, for the first time in her life, is addressed by a delivery boy as "Ma'am"; it absolutely freaks her out. She'd just been "ma'am deflowered".)

Was Mary's delivery boy being "insensitive" by "jumping the miss-ma'am gun"? Hard to say. Complicating the decision for any addresser is the fact that no guidance whatsoever is offered, from any authoritative source, on when a woman transitions from being addressed more properly as a "Miss" to being over some age line, with "Ma'am" now being appropriate. There *is* no official Miss-Ma'am cutoff. And even if there was, the addresser would still run the risk of misjudging a woman's age from her appearance. What a problem for someone obliged to address a borderline-age woman!

But not to worry. Your author has a solution. (Don't I always. You should know me by now.) In the same way that "Ms." was created as a brand new word to fill a usage gap, I propose a brand new word to be used in lieu of "Miss" *or* "Ma'am", an option with no age implications. And that word is: "Ma'amiss".

Think of it: with the substitution of this innovative form of address, no longer will you risk shocking a young woman's pride with a first-time "Ma'am" or shattering a mature woman's dignity with a rude "Miss". Even women lacking both pride *and* dignity might appreciate this demonstration of tact—like when a male customer considerately switches to "Slam, bam, thank-you *Ma'amiss*".

VARIETY SHOW

Yes, *variety*—it's "the spice of life", right? (I know, it's not the first time I'm using it in this book; apologies for *my* less than total commitment to variety in usage, but sometimes, to quote Art Carney in *The Honeymooners*, "the phrase just fits.")

Gum Walks

Oh sure, there are some clods who are so truly incompetent that it fairly applies to them that they "can't walk and chew gum at the same time." But don't we also need nuanced variations, to cover those who are challenged, yes, but not quite as severely? How about: "He can't walk and, at the same time, dispose of chewed gum in a proper sidewalk receptacle?" Or, "He can't walk and, at the same time, look out for chewed gum on the sidewalk?"

Finger Rules

There's the famous "Rule of thumb", of course. But other fingers as well could produce their own "rules", which have the potential to enhance our language:

- + "Rule of forefinger": as my mother repeatedly told me, "Don't point at anyone in public."
- + "Rule of middle finger": If you're going to "flip the bird", make sure the flipee is more like a sparrow or a pigeon than a hawk or an eagle.
- + "Rule of ring finger": Advice for a single *woman* in a singles bar or similar environment where you hope to hook up with a single man for a relationship the longevity of which could range anywhere from one night to rest-of-life marriage: *appear to be married* by wearing a wedding band or ring on your left ring finger. The vast majority of *men* in such environments are looking to hook up for a relationship the longevity of which could range anywhere from one night to one week, and by wearing that ring you present as someone perfect to target: an apparently married woman, who couldn't possibly be looking for a potential commitment (let alone marriage) mate (at least, not for anyone new to fill that role anytime soon) and therefore must be interested exclusively in a short-duration casual sex union. Indeed, most men see a married woman as the "holy grail" for a tawdry hookup with little to no chance that the "commitment issue" will even come up for

uncomfortable discussion. And what a thrilling boost to a man's ego to know that she only wants him for his body!

In this manner, by feeding into shallow male preferences, you'll more likely at least get your foot—not to mention other relevant body parts—in the door, and strike up that desired initial conversation, with that attractive candidate who might otherwise have skipped over you. True, if you later "hit it off" [though, as you know, I prefer "hit it on"] with the guy and he then finds out you're not, in fact, married, he might initially be disappointed, but by that time, hopefully, he'll find himself in love? And actually open to some level of commitment?

Detective Sergeant? BBBBB? Confidential comments, please?

+ "Rule of pinky finger": I couldn't come up with a worthy entrant here—something humorous as well as insightful. I briefly toyed with a comment about Mafiosi and pinky rings, but ultimately rejected it. Ideas, anyone? Garysherbell @ gmail.com.

Switcherahhas

Sometimes a brand new and very useful expression can be arrived at simply by reversing a familiar one. Take, for instance, "You can lead a horse to water but you can't make him drink." Makes a good point, doesn't it, in particular about the challenges of marketing? But now reverse it: "You can't get a horse to drink unless you first get him to the water." Don't you agree that this new expression makes an even better point about the challenges of marketing?

MOUTH TIPS

That word you can't think of, but are so close to coming up with, is "on the tip of your tongue", right? Wrong—or at least, not necessarily. It *would* be at that mouth location *if* the word began with a D, G, J, L, N, T or Z.

If, however, the word in question more likely starts with a B, F, M, P, V or W, you might want to go with, "It's on the tip of my *lips*". For all other words, starting with C, H, K, Q, R, S, Y or a vowel, the generic "It's on the tip of my word-generating mouth part", is probably the best you can do, within the bounds of reasonable linguistic accuracy.

This is no trivial matter. If you really want the person you are talking to, to help you come up with the elusive word, it's imperative that you pin down the word's start sound to its one and only mouth location.

FRACTION ACTION

Every fraction referred to in every expression is the fraction "one-half", usually shortened to just "half". You know which ones I mean: to be "half-serious" or "half-kidding" (same thing); a "half-truth"; "half-baked"; "six of one, half dozen of the other"; and so on. Don't you think that for the sake of variety—and more *precise* expression—we could occasionally employ a *different* fraction? (Note that the issue here is the opposite of the one presented by expressions like the previously analyzed "works like a dog", which are *too* general and could use further specificity. Here we tackle expressions which are *too specific*, and would benefit from variations which provide more precise description.)

For example, married guys, in an attempt to lavish high praise on your wife, don't inflexibly refer to her as "my better half"; instead, when applicable, go with "my better *two-thirds*". UNLESS she's visibly overweight and struggling to diet. UNLESS she has a good sense of humor and you're obviously three-quarters joking.

Perhaps the "halfie" most in need of nuanced variation is "half-naked"—and you probably don't know the half of it. [Sorry, couldn't resist working that one in here.] If a guy presents in, say, shorts and a T-shirt, he is, strictly speaking, at least half naked, if not more so, as per his square inches of uncovered skin, what with his head, neck, most of his arms and most of his legs exposed. Yet, he'd likely be regarded as squarely within the confines of "decent attire", and would rarely be pejoratively tagged as "half-naked". No, "half-naked" is reserved for the showiest of dudes—like the one who struts around the beach in that skimpiest of speedos. Who, in the interests of accuracy, should be described not as "half-naked" but as seven-eighths naked, or even eight-ninths, depending, of course, on how much he has to minimally cover. In sum, "half-naked", in actual usage, is barely accurate and at best half-baked.

By far the most intellectually challenging fraction-expression variation revolves around "half-as*ed", which generally means "lackluster", as in a "half-as*ed effort". If you want to indicate that someone's effort is even worse than that—not just lackluster but utterly incompetent—do you go further *down*, to "quarter-as*ed" or *up* to "three-quarter-as*ed"? Logically, it would be worse than half-as*ed to be "one-quarter-as*ed", but since we're talking about the underlying pejorative trait of "acting like an a*s", one could argue that it's actually *worse* than half-as*ed to do something "*three*-quarter-as*ed". Which way to go?

Okay, so maybe this question is not as philosophically momentous as "Which came first, the chicken or the egg?", but I do think it sure beats "Why did the chicken cross the road"?

POO-POO AND NO-NO

There's no reason English users should be limited to just two "poos" and two "nos". If we want to say that something should be minimized in the extreme, we should be able to "poo-poo-*poo*" it. By the same verbal token, we should be able to claim that something is so categorically forbidden that it's a "no-no-*no*".

For example, suppose the risks of a certain action were at first greatly downplayed, and as a result, it was only mildly forbidden. But then, when the dangers of the action became more apparent, the action was even more strongly prohibited. So it went from a "poo-poo-poo-no-no" to a "poo-poo-no-no-no".

Here's a homework exercise for you readers. What would a "no-poo-poo-no-no" scenario mean? Answers to: garysherbell @ gmail.com.

BRINGING UP THE REAR

… Wherein I devote my attention to three words: "Ass"[5], "Kiss" and "Hole". Dual combinations—"ass-hole" and "ass-kisser"—need no discussion here. But are there ways to combine *all three,* for the sake of enriching our language? Let's get creative:

+ "Ass-hole kisser": (1) someone who likes to kiss people who are ass-holes, OR (2) someone who likes to kiss the ass-hole portion of the ass, OR (3) someone who kisses like an ass-hole.

+ "Ass-hole ass-kisser": (1) ass-kisser who acts like an ass-hole, OR (2) ass-kisser who likes to kiss the ass-hole portion of the ass, OR (3) ass-kisser who kisses the ass of ass-holes.

+ "Ass-hole ass-hole kisser": (1) someone who acts like an ass-hole when he kisses someone who is an ass-hole, OR (2) someone who acts like an ass-hole when he kisses the ass-hole portion of an ass.

A plethora of other enriching options emerge when "ass-hole" is switched to its homonym, "ass-*whole*". For example… Oh, sorry, class! The bell has just rung. We'll have to take that variation up next week.

MY WORD

It's about time Keenan Wynn got his due. In the movie *Dr. Strangelove* he plays a U.S. Army Colonel who famously warns a Peter Sellers character (he plays three in the film) not to commit any "preversions".

Of course, at the time, we all had a good laugh at this comical malapropism, a twist on the real word "*per*version".

---

[5] From hereon, I am dispensing with spelling "Ass" with an asterisk. Decorous comportment must yield to smooth reading. Plus, I'll be striking a bl*w for free speech.

Perhaps, after decades of hindsight, we can finally acknowledge that Mr. Wynn was actually on to something—that while "preversion" is not a word in English, it damn well *ought* to be, because usage-wise, it makes perfect sense. It can and should be used to describe the actions of someone who is on the verge of *becoming* a pervert, but isn't there yet—a "prevert". Like a "prediabetic".

So, then, not a "malapropism" at all, but a "benepropism" (which word, I agree, would technically, ironically, be a "malapropism" itself, as it is a switcheroo on "malapropism".)

I've come up with other "benepropisms" which ought to be in use. Making a "post" word out of a "pre" word is a particularly fertile ground for such creative language enhancement. For example, how about "postposterous"? It would mean, when something appears to be preposterous, only *after* it happens, with the benefit of hindsight. Useful, right? Indeed, the *word* "postposterous" might have initially seemed "preposterous", but now that I've explained it, it doesn't seem postposterous at all, does it.

And how about these "post-ers", which vary off the "pre" version:

+ "postdict": when you fail to predict something, but then dishonestly claim afterward that you did.
+ "posttext": coming up, only *after* you did something, with a reason for doing it.
+ "posteminent": someone who used to be preeminent but is now way past his or her prime.
+ "postvent": to go back in time to prevent from happening something that has already happened. (Sound like a good movie?)
+ "postvail": not instead of "prevail" but in addition to it. "Postvail" should mean what "prevail" now means—to emerge victorious from a conflict—since you can't possibly tell if you've so emerged until *after* the conflict is over. "Prevail" can remain in usage to mean being the one thought most likely to succeed *before* the conflict has begun—in other words, the betting favorite going in.
+ "prepone": which many would say is the better way to say what

"postpone" attempts to say, since the change in timing for an event, to a later time, must obviously occur *in advance*. On the other hand, some might counter that "postpone" is nonetheless to be preferred, since the event in question has been shifted to a time *later* than originally planned. How about a compromise: "prepostpone"?

Hey, readers! Come up with your own "benepropisms". I'm all ears—as well as all *eyes*, if you email me at: garysherbell @ gmail.com.

BY THE NUMBERS

I assume most of you know the significance of the number "69" in human interaction. If you don't, sorry: I WILL NOT SULLY THE DIGNITY OF THIS SCHOLARLY TOME BY PROVIDING AN EXPLANATION. You'll just have to seek it out at your local pool room, singles bar or brothel. Or in the offices of a D.C. lobbyist.

Of relevance here isn't the underlying meaning of this number-expression, but the example it sets of deriving an expression from the sheer physical appearance of a number's digits.

Perhaps it is our obsession with sex which accounts for why, so far, only this one "dirty" expression has been so derived. I, on the other hand, will not be so creatively encumbered. Here are some others to consider—all applying to intimate human interactions, yes, but reasonably clean:

+ "55": what my girlfriend and I call it when we face each other, usually bare from the waist up, usually lying down, and simultaneously scratch each other's back. My 5 fingers and her 5 fingers both engaged at the same time in doing the same thing to the other.
+ "22": in the same numerical vein, when my girlfriend and I kiss each other on the lips: my two on her two.
+ "77": when you and another do "55" and "22" at the same time.

Hey, Melbourne Sheep-Herder's Wife: consider trying these techniques with your husband. Might even help you fall asleep.

CLEANING UP

While we're on the subject of clean vs. dirty…

Have you noticed how many words there are in English which have a perfectly clean usage, but also a dirty one? With a sexual or scatological connotation? Words like "ass", or "nuts", or "dick", or "prick", or "stool", or "balls", or "cock", or "blow", or "suck", or "hard", or "breast"….?

This is not an insignificant problem—especially for teachers. Try teaching a class in biology to twelve-year-olds, and mention the "titmouse", and see how many disruptive—well, *titters* you get—especially from the boys. I assure you, it won't be the "mouse" part of the word which sets them off. (Now that I think of it, is it possible that the very word, "titter" is somehow derived from "tit"? Something to research.)

That same teacher would face a similar discomforting eruption when mentioning "cock", in the chicken context, or "ass" in the donkey context. In an English class, any reference to "breast" in a poem could lead to immature response problems. Gym teachers have always had to contend with "balls" taken the wrong way. And history teachers have often been wary when referring to a particular former president as "Dick Nixon". Of course, in all cases, I'm talking about classes with students below the high school level. Still, that's enough of a student population to present a formidable scholastic challenge.

The remedy here is obvious: to come up with new and different words for the so-called "dirty" uses—like "cuck" instead of "cock" (which has precedent, as a matter of fact, in the word "cuckold".) The hope would be that eventually the use of "cuck" would supplant "cock", in the sexual context, so that junior high school biology teachers could then, for example, describe a rooster's "cock-a-doodle-do" without running the risk of a raucous classroom reverberation.

That's just one suggestion for change to get you reform-minded folks started. But that's as far as I'll go—and it's not just because of space limitations. It's because—I admit, in the interests of full disclosure—that I am of two minds about such reform. Sure, I'd like to help the teachers, but as a comedy writer, I would be adversely affected by such systemic word replacements, and might therefore be opposed to such changes, purely out of self-interest. The fact that many English words have a second "dirty" meaning happens to be a source of much comedy. So I'm conflicted here; I'm not too keen on throwing out the comedy baby with the reform bathwater.[6]

Here's just one example of the anti-comedic potential of such reforms: the late, great George Carlin once famously, and derisively, said, on the subject of censorship, that "On TV you can say you 'pricked your finger', but you can't say you 'fingered your prick'." Good one, George! Now, I ask you, readers, where would that joke be if "prick" didn't have those dual meanings?

Recently, I even came up with my own joke that relies on clean/dirty dual meanings. See what you think of it (comments welcome):

Julius Cesar once famously said, "I came, I saw, I conquered." But that's not what he originally said. The Roman Me-Too (Me-Tu?) activists got to him and forced him to change it to that. Originally, it was "I saw, I conquered, I came."

Yup, with the Comedy Lobby aligned in opposition, it could be a while before English "cleans up its act."

MAXIM FUSION

---

[6] I know, I know, I did lampoon this expression. But my girlfriend is a fan of this one—she uses it all the time. So I decided to use it myself in this book, at least once, just to show her that I'm open-minded and not unrealistically doctrinaire on usage issues.

Community of English speakers: Let's put all our heads together and create useful new idiomatic expressions *by combining two or more already in use.* Here are some of my own suggestions, with a brief explanation for each: what it would mean and how it might be employed.

- "Cold feet shoulder": What happens when you have second thoughts about giving someone the cold shoulder.
- "Hit the hay roll": When two people get it on casually, then immediately fall asleep together.
- "Scaredy cats have nine lives": Another way of saying, "Discretion is the better part of valor."
- "Goodbye goodtime Charlie": Someone who has too much of a good time too often, risking a premature final "goodbye".
- "Robbing Peter to pay Paul, for Pete's sake": Peter actually owes Paul the money, so in the end, justice is done—while saving Peter's soul.
- "Adding insult to shooting yourself in the foot": Your proposed remedy backfires on you, and your critics won't let you forget it.
- "A taste of your own medicinal cure worse than the disease": You (1) propose a medicinal cure for a disease and (2) after you get the disease yourself (3) you try your proposed cure and (4) find out that your proposed cure is worse than the disease. It could happen.
- "Ruffling the feathers in your cap": Someone publicly challenges your recognized accomplishments.
- "Speaking of the Devil in the details": Those troubling little details keep coming back to haunt you, again and again.
- "Sitting ducks in a row": "Sitting" ducks are easier to shoot than flying ones. So are ducks "in a row". Now imagine they are sitting *and* in a row. A duck-hunter's dream!
- "A chip off the old block on your shoulder": The chip's on your shoulder because of some grievance your *father* had. (True, I did say earlier that a "chip on one's shoulder" was highly unlikely—but possible for brief periods of time.)
- "Back to square one on the drawing board": "Back to the drawing board" is unclear about how much usable work is still left on the

board; "back to square one" is unclear whether you are involved in a creative project, or just some game, like *Monopoly*. Combining the two cures both expression gaps.

+ "Putting your best foot forward by putting it down": Improving your chances of, say, getting a new job or a promotion, by decisively refusing to go along with a job condition—impressively demonstrating your mettle.
+ "We'll cross that bridge when we come to it—and not burn it": Make your decision on whether to cross the bridge when you get to it—but don't burn the bridge after you cross, so you can go back across, if you realize you made the wrong decision.
+ "Love-nest egg": What a scheming woman gets when she parlays being a rich man's mistress into a generous financial settlement.
+ "My my word": Combining "My my" and "My word" to show an unusual degree of surprise.
+ "Don't let the cat out of the bag, or else, out of curiosity, it may well eat the canary, in the coal mine, causing a gas explosion": combining *three* catty expressions. True, not likely to be of much utility. Still, I couldn't resist including it, as a mental exercise in maximum maxim fusion.

But I'm not finished! Did I just say "maximum"? How about ... *five?* As in:

+ "Wishy-washy riff-raff wheeler-dealer hanky-panky flim-flam": When a mediocre low-class fast operator uses trickery to commit fraud. (Is there a way to squeeze in "mumbo-jumbo" here and make it an even half-dozen? L.A. Playwright?)

SECTION 2 — PROGRESSIVE PROGRESS

Let's make the evolution of English work for us, as we compassionately pursue truth, honesty, justice, equality, equity, diversity, democracy, freedom and a stable climate. (Did I leave out anything good?)

ANTI-LEFT BIAS

Sorry to say, bias against the left-handed is rife in our English language. (Full disclosure: I am right-handed.) There's the "left-handed compliment", which in a subtle way, is actually critical, not the compliment it purports to be. Or there's describing a poor dancer as having "two left feet". (Why not two *right* feet?) And how about "the left hand doesn't know what the right hand is doing"? (Why is the left hand stigmatized as the "ignorant" one, which isn't keeping proper tabs on the other hand?)

Sometimes the language bias is indirect, taking the form of *favoring* the right-handed. For example, having to say, "I'd give my right arm" for something really good—even if you're actually left-handed. Or referring to a boss's key aide as his or her "right-hand man"—even if the boss is left-handed. Or how about when you're being asked to swear to tell the truth; invariably you are first asked to "raise your right hand." Why not the left hand? Or at least, "Raise a hand of your choice"?

Speaking of raising a hand, readers, raise your hand—left *or* right—if, after reading the title of this passage, you assumed it would be about bias against the *political* left. Hmmm ... that was dumb of me. I can't *see* any of you. Okay, I'll just have to assume that most of you raised a hand.

Fact is, "left" as pertaining to a political persuasion has nothing whatsoever to do with left-handedness. I do know a thing or two about 18th Century French history (not bragging; I said "a thing or two"—not three or more) and if memory serves, the term was derived from the fact that certain persons, with positions we now consider "leftist", were seated on the left side of a new legislative body in the early days of the French Revolution.

Still, that doesn't mean that we should simply ignore this demonstration of blatant bias against the left-handed—even if it is confined entirely to our language. Constituting only about ten percent of the U.S. population, the left-handed certainly do qualify as a "minority". Which means they are entitled to our protection from any and all forms of discrimination. Furthermore, allowing this language bias against the left-handed to continue in our lingo would set a dangerous precedent, which could lead to greater tolerance of similar bias in our language against other minorities.

Going forward, it is imperative that we replace all of those insensitive "left-biased" expressions with neutral-handed versions. To make this happen, we must all march together in protest—hand-in-hand, which obviously means, one person's left hand holding another person's right. Forward! United! Right on!... Er... Ummm... Left on!? ... Er... ummm... Wait! I got it!: *Hands* on!

PERSONOUNS

Who'd ever think that a boring subject like English pronouns could become a hot-button issue in today's English-speaking world? Well, it has become one.

Since its inception, English has suffered from a usage gap in that there is no non-gender-specific third-person pronoun. It's either a "he" or a "she", and if you don't want to be gender-specific, you have to go with the cumbersome "he or she" or "he/she". Gosh, how many times in this very book have I had to go through that grammarigamarole?

Wouldn't it have been simpler if, after all these centuries, English had developed a generic third person singular pronoun? And that includes, a generic form to replace the possessives "his" or "hers" or the whatchamacallits "him" or "her"? The fact that there still is none of these is about as crazy as the previously discussed facts that "inflammable" means the same as "flammable" or the spelling of "phlegm".

Enter modern progressivism, with its revulsion at what is called "gender binarism"—that is, using *any* gender identification for a third person pronoun, on the theory that many people are neither male nor female, and cannot be neatly categorized as one or the other. Even "he or she" is verboten to these language hawks. Their solution is to go with the only non-gender-specific pronoun available: "they" (or "their" or "them" in the other pronoun tenses.) Which non-progressives object to on the ground that it's a *plural* pronoun, which is confusing when you're talking about a single person, of whatever gender.

Of course, a solution all would be happy with is to come up with that long-sought non-gender-specific third person singular pronoun. Fine—maybe that will happen someday. But until then?

Perhaps you thought that as the author of this work I'd be offering some ideas on possible new pronouns to fill this role. But I make no such offer. Actually, I was hoping that you readers could come up with some worthy ideas. Please forward them to: garysherbell @ gmail.com.

In fact, if anyone thinks I'm going to weigh in on this issue at all, and take one cancellation-risking side, boy-oh-boy, and girl-oh-girl, is he or she—or they—crazy.

One final note: I've given this subsection the title "personouns". As far as I know, that's an original creation of mine. But is it? Has anyone used it before? I wonder. Do tell.

WEATHER OR NOT

To educate those not yet woke on the climate change crisis (as well as those not yet at the highest woke stage: missing-sleep-from-worry), we need to constantly remind people of the weather—especially *bad* weather.

For example, when talking about rain, always try to find a way to slip in the observation, "When it rains, it pours". And when asked whether you will be attending a certain event, don't reply merely that you are coming "Rain or shine". Instead, expand your reply to: "I'm coming, rain or shine, flood or drought, wind or calm, clear or fog, monsoon or hurricane," thus taking the opportunity to fully remind the listener of all the many ill-effects of climate change which are on the verge of destroying Earth.

Furthermore, we should be making greater use of all those expressions which collaterally pertain to bad weather. In other words—literally— never say, "The same thing is unlikely to happen again"; instead say, "Lightening doesn't strike twice in the same place". And never say, "You took the words right out of my mouth"; always say, when applicable, "You're stealing my thunder". And don't say, "You're spoiling my good time"; instead go with, "Don't rain on my parade". And when you want to say that there's little chance of something happening, you have *two* weathery choices: "When Hell freezes over", or "A snowball in Hell". Finally, when you're not well, and someone asks you how you are, don't fail to say that you're "Under the weather". And if you are in fact fine, do go out of your way to creatively remark, "I'm *over* the weather". Anything that helps promote weather awareness!

THIS MEANS WAR

Many progressives are demanding that certain U.S. military bases, named after Southern Confederate generals, be renamed. I sympathize with where they are coming from, but I fear they are missing the point. Fort names should of course be changed... but *only* when the general was a competent general whose efforts contributed to the South's military success. A fort name should *not* be changed when it's named after a general whose incompetence led to the *losing* of the war, and hence, the freeing of the slaves.

For example, Fort *Bragg* should indeed have its name changed, but not Fort *Pickett*, named in "honor" of the general whose infamously disastrous charge at the Battle of Gettysburg, in July, 1863, "Pickett's Charge", is seen by many historians as a turning point in the war, against the South.

[In fairness to the General, and his descendants, most historians would agree that it was Lee's decision to charge, with Pickett getting all the historical heat.]

DISPANICS

How come gringo Bob always gets acceptance—"Yesiree Bob"—while Latino Jose gets only rejection—"No way Jose"?

And come to think of it, aren't we adding language insult to injury by saying to Jose "No way", instead of "No es posible"?

MALES ON TOP

Not what you're probably thinking, Detective Sergeant.

Most expressions incorporating actual names employ *men's* names: "Joe College", "Good time Charlie", "Jack of all trades", and so on. Not entirely unexpected, is it, given that our society has been male-dominated through most of history.

But societies are no longer male-dominated—or at least, not so much as they used to be. Therefore, isn't it fitting that many of these expressions now be given *female*-oriented variations, for those who prefer to go that more diverse route?

Here, as an example, is just one revision to consider, with political overtones: how about revising "Robbing Peter to pay Paul" to "Robbing Peter to pay *Paula*"? In addition to offering greater gender diversity, the revised expression also suggests the propriety of a kind of Robinhoodish *reparations*, with Paula getting money from Peter—money she perhaps actually deserves. Want to be strictly legal about such reparation transfers? Then how about: "*Taxing* Peter to pay Paula?"

As for female variations which are entirely missing, perhaps none is more glaring than in the realm of male "bathroom language": no female counterparts for "the John" (the male bathroom), "a John" (a male prostitute customer) and the "Johnson" (a male sexual organ.) Some women might prefer it that way—no female counterparts—while others would want to at least have them, on record, if only for equal opportunity. For those women, should we go with "Mary" as the natural equivalent of "John"? If so, then "the Mary" would be the woman's bathroom, "a Mary" would be a woman who seeks the services of a gigolo, and the female sexual organ would be…? What? The "Maryland"? With all due respect to the residents of Baltimore.

BEAT THE TOM-TOM

I don't make it a practice to go to bat for groups of people who, though being unfairly treated, as a group, have not been recognized as "historically marginalized". I will now make an exception: for all men named "Tom". That name has mercilessly taken it on the chin in expression-land, what with how often it is used in a pejorative context. From "peeping Tom" to "doubting Thomas", to "Uncle Tom", to "Tomfoolery", to "tomboy", to weapons like the "tomahawk" and the "Tommy gun"… Just about the best "Tom" can do here is be presented as ordinary, as in "Tom, Dick and Harry".

Frankly, I'm surprised—and disappointed—that celebrity Toms, like Cruise and Hanks, haven't yet gone public with any complaint about this shabby verbal treatment—and with suggestions for reform. Well, if they won't, I will. I propose that we gradually replace the use of the above "Tom" expressions with—or at least make dual use of—ones using other male names in its place, like:

+ Instead of "peeping Tom", "peeping Isaac", cleverly incorporating the "eye" sound.
+ Instead of "Tomboy", "Patboy", progressively substituting with the neutral gendered "Pat".
+ Instead of "Uncle Tom", "Uncle Fred"—since I know at least one Black dude named "Fred" who's kissed more white ass than any

Black "Tom" I know.
+ Instead of "Doubting Thomas", "Doubting Gary", named after yours truly. And why not, considering how broadly I've been doubting all those English language usages we've for so long taken for granted.

BOWEL HOWLS

It's often not a good idea to wait until organized groups go public with their criticisms of perceived insensitive expressions. Sometimes we need to anticipate such criticisms by beginning to appreciate the harm such expressions have been causing, which we have been so far unaware of. Then, accordingly, discontinue the use of that expression, at least publicly.

One such insensitive expression, which hasn't yet garnered the *public* attention it well deserves, for making light of persons with certain disabilities, is "Tough sh*t".

Now I do understand that this expression is a very popular one, used often to conveniently and concisely convey to another, who has suffered a setback: "Sorry, welcome to the real cruel world."

But a history of longtime utilitarian use is simply no defense—at least, not anymore. It's now clear to me that people suffering from such conditions as chronic constipation and irritable bowel syndrome have all along been quite offended by the persistent employment of this callous expression, which alludes to their disability merely to make a motivational point. I wouldn't be surprised if lobby groups representing persons with bowel ailments are already primed to soon go public with their displeasure.

So take heed. You've been forewarned. My advice is to begin phasing out the use of this expression *now*. For if you complacently continue to use it, waiting for its critics to go public, you may be too late to avoid serious consequences. Do you want to be the first one cancelled through such an organized effort? Don't count on a belated apology to save your—well, *ass*.

If you do end up losing your job, or suffer some other cancellation indignity, don't expect any sympathy from me. All you'll get from yours truly is a big, fat "I told you so." Or better yet, a "Tough sh*t!" (Not witnessed, recorded or in writing.)

ADDENDUM: EVERYONE TALKS ABOUT THE WEATHER

At this time, permit me to somewhat modify what I said earlier about constantly striving for weather consciousness to promote climate change awareness. I would like to add:

Of course, we don't want to overdo it and turn off some independent, open-minded thinkers on this vital subject with incessant weather talk. As Mark Twain didn't, but might well have said, "Everyone talks about the weather, but nobody does anything about them."

SECTION 3—TOWARDS A MORE HONEST DISCOURSE

If we English speakers and writers want English to evolve beneficially, then we must do our part with improved *usage*. Many of the problems in the current use of English are not the fault of the language, per se, but of how we have chosen to *employ* it.

One major fault is—well, I wouldn't say, *dis*honesty so much as I'd say *inadequate honesty*. When it comes to English usage, honesty should be the best verbal policy. I recall someone once saying in a film, "I say what I mean, and I mean what I say." I apologize for not doing enough film research to be more specific, but no matter the actor and film, those words remain a sound communication attitude.

Here are some examples of what I mean—human interactions where there's a crying need for more honest discourse…

OFFENSE? YOU BETCHA

In the course of saying something offensive to me, people often add "No offense". Perhaps at the tail end, as a courtesy afterthought, or even in the beginning, as a preface, as in, "No offense, but—." In either case, their "no offense disclaimer" is an obvious non-truth: they're offending me, and they damn well know it. And they know that *I* know it. I say to them: bad enough you're offending me; please don't compound the offense by insulting my intelligence. Just offend me, and leave it at that.

RESPECT? NADA

… And don't think you're going to weasel out of your honesty responsibilities by switching to "With all due respect". Means the same thing! Same lame claim! Same insult to my intelligence! If you truly respected me, you wouldn't be saying it! How about a strictly honest, "I don't respect you, and here's why…"?

Channeling Rodney Dangerfield and Aretha Franklin on this point. (If you don't get my allusions to these two show-biz luminaries, sorry. With all due respect, try doing an internet search on them.)

AND WHAT IF I DO?

Here's another super-irker: when people say, "If you don't mind…" at the same moment as they do the very thing they were inquiring about, which I damn well *might* have minded but hadn't been given enough time to object to!

Why, this very same thing happened to me, not too long ago, when I was seated at a desk, pen in hand, and a woman standing before me suddenly grabbed the pen out of my hand, to write something down, just as she said, "If you don't mind…". Of course, I didn't *particularly* mind, and didn't make an issue out of it. In fact, I put a smile on my face as we laughed about it, while I politely explained to her that I *might* have minded, but hadn't been given enough time to formally register any objection.

Next time you try this mistimed courtesy, you might not be so lucky in getting a non-combative response. My recommendation: a "three-second rule": after saying your obligatory "If you don't mind", and making clear your goal (by, say, pointing to the pen) wait three seconds before actually going ahead with your planned action. Why three? There's a "three-second rule" in basketball, governing how long you can remain in a certain area under the basket, and that seems to work, so…?

JUST ASK

Another expression where the timing is out of whack is when you say, "I'm going to have to ask you to…", wherein you are apparently, and yes, dishonestly, stating that you are *going* to ask someone, in the future, to do something, when it is actually your intention that your statement be taken as a request *now*—signed, sealed and delivered.

I understand where you, as the asker, are coming from: you probably feel kind of guilty for having to ask it, and want to make sure the askee understands that you make the request only reluctantly, perhaps following someone else's orders. Furthermore, since it pains you to make the request, starting with a pointless "I'm going to have to ask you" instead of plunging right ahead to the request, buys you more time, putting off the painful duty, if only for a few more seconds.

I highly recommend that, as the asker, you get right to it, and don't adopt this namby-pamby approach of saying "I'm going to have to ask you to...".

As an example, let's go back to that upstairs neighbor playing the tuba. Do not say to him, "I'm going to have to ask you to stop playing the tuba." Rather, say, "I'm asking you to stop playing the tuba"—at least making it clear that you are *now* asking, not merely stating that you *will* be doing so in the future. Or even better: "Stop playing the tuba." (Though you might want to conclude with a softening "Please".)

The direct approach could make a critical difference in whether you get the tuba player to stop. Pussyfooting around with "I'm going to..." could unstrategically demonstrate a degree of weakness in your resolve and embolden him to stand his ground and *not* stop.

Police officers have to be particularly careful in their choice of words and should rarely use the weaker "I'm going to have to ask you to...". (I wonder if you'll agree with me, Detective Sergeant.) If, for example, a citizen is standing where he or she ought not, and as an officer you come up to him (or her) and say, "I'm going to have to ask you to move," the citizen could rightfully stand his or her ground and *not* move, saying something like, "Go ahead." You might then say, "I told you to move!" And the citizen could rightfully then say, "No you didn't. You said you were *going* to have to ask me to move. Fine. I'm still waiting for you to do so." Now that you've realized your verbal mistake, you could go on to directly state, to the technically correct wiseass, "Move!" Meanwhile, valuable time has been lost when you could have approached other citizens requiring a similar order.

And, from the point of view of the wi—, er, citizen, be aware that the officer just might now ignore his initial statement altogether, and switch to, "I'm going to have to… punch you in your mouth." Or more directly, might just proceed to punch you in your mouth. Ah, such are the risks we must take to linguistically stand up for our civil liberties!

Judge, perhaps you'd like to wade into the legal issues presented here. I said that, in my view, the citizen could rightfully not yet move, because the officer only said he was "going" to ask him to. But, on second thought, could the citizen's refusal, on a linguistic technicality—when he obviously knew, or should have known, what the officer actually meant—constitute obstruction of governmental operations?

HOW ARE YOU NOT

Probably the one question you've received more often than any other, thus far in your life, is "How are you"? Or its close cousin, "How are you doing?" [We are talking here of the expression emanating from someone you already know, not from someone you are meeting for the first time—as previously discussed.] And if you're like me, then every single time you hear it, you're in a quandary as to how to respond. Problem is, the asker could have meant either of two vastly different things: (1) a throwaway line substitute for "Hello" or "Hi"; or (2) a genuine inquiry as to your condition: how you are feeling, how you are getting along, and so on.

If the asker is encountered in passing, and hastily continues on, right past you, then obviously option one was intended. Or, if you've been known to have recently experienced, say, a bad illness, or a death in the family, and the asker emphasizes the "are" word, as in, "How ARE you?", you can reasonably assume a genuine inquiry was intended.

But what to do when neither advance clue applies, and you then find yourself standing right next to the person? Do you assume that option one was intended—a throwaway "hello"—and merely nod, or grunt an equally fake "fine", or maybe even echo with a similarly dishonest "How are you?" of your own? Last thing you want to do is take the question seriously and launch unnecessarily into a boring, self-centered speech on your condition, not remotely asked for or expected—which will not be appreciated one bit by the asker, whom you might hardly know. On the other hand, if the asker actually was, genuinely, inquiring as to your condition, your responding as if it was just a "Hello" could be taken as unfriendly, with you coming across as cold and distant.

Solutions, anyone? Here's one—the only one I can think of, courtesy of yours truly, your Grim English Reaper: LET'S ALL STOP SAYING "HOW ARE YOU" OR "HOW ARE YOU DOING" AS A SUBSTITUTE FOR "HELLO".

To facilitate this transition away from the problematic usage, do what I do. When people say "How are you" and I'm pretty sure all they meant was a "Hello", I verbally punish the person by purporting to take the question as a serious inquiry, replying with, "Well, actually, at the moment, my ears are full of wax," or "As a matter of fact—thanks for asking—I'm hearing some strange rumbling in my stomach." Or if you really want to embarrass the asker for his or her dishonest hello, launch into something like, "How am I? How do you mean? Could you be more specific? Do you mean emotionally? Or psychologically? Or spiritually? Or financially? Or physically? And if it's the physical you want to know about, do you mean cardiovascular? Gastrointestinal? Sexual?"

You can be sure, that asker will never direct a throwaway-Hello "How are you" at you again—or at anyone else, either.

Anyone willing to join with me in what so far has been a one-person crusade?

BIRTHDAY GREETINGS

The customary exclamation bestowed upon someone when learning that it is that person's birthday is "Happy Birthday!"

It's probably been that way for centuries—or even millennia. A reassessment of this usage is long overdue. Does this exclamation actually comport with the mood of most birthday persons? Is the so-called celebrant actually "happy" about the event? That is, happy about now being recognized as one year older?

To answer this question it is useful—if not imperative—to go back to the time when the birthday greeting tradition began. Or at least imagine its likely origins:

OOG: Chief, my mother says that I was born on this same date 18 suns ago.

MOOG (THE TRIBAL CHIEF): So then, Oog, today is what we now call your "birth" day.

OOG: Yes, so they say. Today I am 18 suns old.

MOOG: 18 *years* old, as we now say. And as we also now say, "Happy Birthday!"

OOG: "Happy" birthday? I haven't heard that one before.

MOOG: Shmoog came up with that one, about a moon ago.

OOG: Why "happy"? Now that I'm 18, I must go off to battle with the Mountain People. And must settle down with a woman to have children. No more hanging out at the campfires with the guys on Friday nights.

MOOG: As the Chief, I am always looking to beef up our Warriors by adding another strong young man—like you. And as you know, my older sister, Droog, still has no mate, and so still no children. I was hoping you and she ...

(OOG does not reply, only looks down, awkwardly.)

MOOG (Cont.): You could do worse, you know. The Chief's sister...

OOG (Looks up, trying to put on a brave face): Well, if you put it that way...

MOOG: So, while *you* might not be "happy" today, Oog, *I* certainly am. Happy Birthday!

AUTHOR: Times have changed. We no longer have a draft, at least in the U.S.. And no one is forced to marry when reaching a certain age. So who's to be "happy" just because someone has a birthday?

L.A. Playwright, just a friendly reminder: the above material is copyrighted.

SECTION 4—OUR LIVING LANGUAGE

Or is it dying? From disturbing current trends? The persistence of cliches which have long overstayed their welcome, the degradation of meaning, and the use of one-size-fits-all catchphrases, totally lacking in nuance…?

Here are my biggest gripes—or as I like to say, Sherbellyaches—which raise concerns about the very survival of our glorious language…

ENOUGH ALREADY

That's right, using a cliché to fight cliches! (I would have gone with "Enough is enough" but I've already critiqued that one.)

Cliches present an issue of quantity, not quality. Most are initially welcomed as "fresh", but eventually suffer from the disability of overuse, which dulls their descriptive bite. Time to move on. As with…

Duh
By now, way overdone as a response to something stated which is all-too obvious or self-evident.

I know, I know, some of you alert readers who'd be all-too happy to nail me on a Hypocrisy would be quick to point out that I've used it myself, in this book, even once as a *section-heading* no less. My defense: I used it *before* I critiqued it.

Spot On
A more decorous way to show your agreement than the acerbic "Duh": calmly indicating that a statement you agree with is "spot on". But ready for the English Usage Retirement Home, don't you think? Okay, perhaps with one exception: could still be used to explain what happens to your shirt when you eat spaghetti.

D'ya Think?
Initially I wasn't going to include this item, but when writing the above passage, which contains "do you think", it occurred to me that a more vitriolic form of this question—"*D'ya think*"—has been used often, of late, to indicate (like "Duh"), that something is especially obvious. If not yet an overdone cliché, it's something to keep our cliché-hunter eyes and ears on.

24 Times 7
"24 and 7" has been in use for quite a while now to indicate "24 hours a day and 7 days a week"—a way for, say, a store to get across that they are open at all times.

Now, this expression does perform an invaluable service, filling a linguistic niche, so I'm not about to suggest chucking it altogether—overused though it may be—*unless* a satisfactory replacement is immediately available. And I do have one. Multiply 24 by 7 and what do you get? Why, *168*, the total number of hours in a week—thus meaning precisely the same as "24 and 7". (Do check my math, Hong Kong Banker.)

Furthermore, "168" contains only *four* syllables, while "24 and 7" contains *six* (50 percent more—again check my math, Hong Kong Banker), so 168 has the added advantage of superior brevity. Okay, for nostalgic reasons, we might not want to fully retire "24 and 7" for all time; but can we at least give it a rest and go with "168" for a while?

UNLIKE LIKE

What's not to like about the ubiquitous "Like"? If you, like, must know: like, alot.

Have I already made my point? In the first place, using that word that way is a lazy cop out. Instead of being detailed and specific in describing something, the "like" option allows you to get away with just a very general description of it. Much harder now to accuse you of inaccuracy when all you're warranting is that the described item has a "rough similarity" to something else.

It's like—and you'll appreciate this, Judge—a witness testifying in court as to his or her overall *impression*, rather than far more credibly to the detailed observations which led to that impression. For example: stating, "He was, like, angry at me", instead of stating, "He was red in the face, gritted his teeth and significantly raised his voice."

Above, I said "In the first place..." So there must be a "second place", right? Well, there is: after the pervasive, persistent usage of the "cop out 'like'", for all these years, it's simply become ... *cliched*. Like those other cliché culprits in the previous section. It's time for a *varied* way of saying the same thing—even if it doesn't solve the problem of lack of detail and specificity. How about "similar to"? Which would lead us to, "He was, similar to, angry at me." Or for bold variety, how about turning the positive into a negative? As in, "He was, *un*like, happy with me."

Variety can be and should be an end in itself. I mean, isn't "variety the spice of life?"... Hmmm... I believe I already used that line more than once in this book... So I guess, for the sake of—well, *variety*, I'll have to replace it... I'll get back to you all on that...

CARING, MORE OR LESS

Don't get me started on this one... Too late...

It's absolutely outrageous to me that so many people, including highly educated ones, lazily say, "I could care less"—which literally means that you *do* care—when it is their fully understood intention to state that they are at *rock bottom* on the caring scale, and therefore *should* be saying, "I *couldn't* care less." The complete opposite of what they said!

What is particularly troubling to me is how rarely—if ever—the *listener* corrects the speaker's language error, even when the listener well knows a grievous gaffe has been committed.

What I'm seeing here is evidence of the creeping degradation of the English language. Which does not bode well for its future.

If I sound really angry, it's because I COULD CARE LESS! That means, I DO care, get it? Am I getting through to y'all?

WHATEVER

You knew this one was coming, didn't you—the *Jaws* of all reviled word creatures, the word perennially voted as the most despised for its harmful and nondeserving ubiquity.

Like "like", "whatever" is also now being used, all over, as a vague cop-out, in place of far more descriptive phrases, sentences and sometimes even whole paragraphs, that heretofore might have been employed. The vastly more detailed, and colorful, replaced by the same cookie-cutter one-word alternative.

I fully understand that Whateverism can never be totally eradicated. It's just too damn convenient to use this single word instead of a whole lot of other words. Brevity does count for alot in this time-challenging world.

But I believe that there is a way for us to "have our language cake and eat it too": by sticking with "whatever", but adding a simple *number* to it, to indicate which phrase, sentence or paragraph it is replacing. Like: "Whatever-One", "Whatever-Two", "Whatever-Three", etc. Thus retaining the benefit of brevity, while regaining some of the expressiveness lost with the switch to a mere "whatever".

Of course, we cannot create a "numbered whatever" for every conceivable replacement candidate—only for the ones which are commonly intended when "whatever" is used in its place.

This "Whatever Number Project" would probably need a team effort to succeed. Perhaps you six Advance Copy Recipients—Judge, L.A. Playwright, BBBBB, Liverpool Detective Sergeant, Hong Kong Banker and Melbourne Sheep-Herder's Wife—could work with me on this?

Below, to get us all started, is my own preliminary list of phrases, sentences and whole paragraphs which have been largely—and regrettably—replaced by "Whatever":

+ "I have no idea."
+ "If you say so."
+ "I have no comment."
+ "That doesn't interest me at all."
+ "This whole discussion bores me."
+ "I don't know what to say."
+ "I'm tired of you asking me that."
+ "I'm not the right person to ask."
+ "I couldn't care less." (Or, by mistake, "I could care less".)
+ "Huh? Oh, forget it."
+ "I'm too busy to talk about it right now."
+ "Didn't you just say that? You're repeating yourself."
+ "There's nothing we can do about it anyway, so…"
+ "Please stop bothering me with this nonsense."
+ "You're missing the point and I don't want to talk about it anymore."
+ "That's a ridiculous thing to say and I won't even respond."
+ "I didn't hear what you just said. Could you repeat that? Wait… on second thought… Never mind."
+ "You didn't bother to read my book so why should I answer you."
+ "Since you might be recording this conversation, my honest answer could get me in trouble."
+ "Well, that's just too damn bad, you hypocrite, but I wouldn't dare tell you that to your face."
+ "I know what you're trying to do: draw me into a discussion you know I don't want. Well, I'm not falling into your trap."
+ "The last time you said that was at that party, remember? What a diss! I told you so at the time. But here you are, at it again. What would be the point of my giving you the same reply?"

Now I say to each of you Six, please do come up with your own list. Then we'll work on it together: combining our lists into one final list, and numbering each on the list as "Whatever-One", "Whatever-Two", and so on, down the list. To facilitate this effort, I suppose it would be best if we all met someday. Wherever. Whenever.

<u>FINISHED</u>

About the Author

Gary Sherbell is the author of three published novels. Also a screenwriter and a playwright, his stage play version of *Two Suspects* was produced in 2016 at the prestigious Cherry Lane Theatre in NYC. A graduate of NYU Law School, he has been a NYC Administrative Law Judge for over 20 years. He lives in NYC's West Village, but his heart remains buried across the East River in Brooklyn, where he was born and raised. Fittingly, his favorite sitcom is still *The Honeymooners*, and he continues to LOL at every episode, even though he's seen each one over thirty times.

Note from Gary Sherbell

Word-of-mouth is crucial for any author to succeed. If you enjoyed *Damn English!*, please leave a review online—anywhere you are able. Even if it's just a sentence or two. It would make all the difference and would be very much appreciated.

Thanks!
Gary Sherbell

We hope you enjoyed reading this title from:

www.blackrosewriting.com

Subscribe to our mailing list – *The Rosevine* – and receive **FREE** books, daily deals, and stay current with news about upcoming releases and our hottest authors.
Scan the QR code below to sign up.

Already a subscriber? Please accept a sincere thank you for being a fan of Black Rose Writing authors.

View other Black Rose Writing titles at www.blackrosewriting.com/books and use promo code **PRINT** to receive a **20% discount** when purchasing.

www.ingramcontent.com/pod-product-compliance
Lightning Source LLC
Chambersburg PA
CBHW072210070526
44585CB00015B/1267